PRAISE FOR

DEEP LIKE ME

Deep Like Me is a refreshing collection of pithy reflections that stretched my heart and made me laugh out loud. Thank you, Rick, for being authentically *you* and for using your storytelling gift to inspire Jesus followers to reclaim their missional purpose.

LARRY ACOSTA
President and founder of Urban Youth Workers Institute

How refreshing it is when we pull all of the pomp and pious rhetoric out of our Christianity and speak honestly about the simple truths the Father shows us through our daily lives. This book does just that. It presents a witty and often hilarious perspective on the ways we tend to relate to God and each other. As I read this book, I was encouraged and reminded of God's sense of humor in the way He reveals Himself to His children. *Deep Like Me* is lighthearted, yet still challenges the reader to think from Christ's perspective.

TOBIN BAWINKEL
Lead vocalist and guitarist of Flatfoot 56

I knew Rick as a surfer before I knew him as a pastor and writer. Without ever having met me or knowing the recent difficulties my family had been through, Rick quietly fixed me up with a board, picked me up and took me surfing every day of our week-long retreat in Hawaii. Those surfs were therapy! I was sincerely touched by his unfussy open-handedness toward us. Rick was humble, generous, quietly confident in his faith and ready to give his ear and share his time and experiences with us. So, these thoughts on faith come with good pedigree! They are written with refreshing honesty and a disarming irreverence that drew me nearer to the Lord as I read them. I'm sure you will find they do the same for you.

BRENTON BROWN
Worship leader and composer

Rick Bundschuh is a friend, and when I am hanging out with him, I always wish for more time. Just like Rick, this book is challenging, thought-provoking, funny, unique, refreshing and filled with truth. I made a list of people to whom I am going to give this book, including my own three daughters.

JIM BURNS, PH.D.
President of HomeWord and author of *Creating An Intimate Marriage, Confident Parenting* and *The Purity Code*

Rick Bundschuh and I have only spent a few hours together over the course of the last 10 years, but I now understand his mind and soul better than I do people with whom I spend plenty of time. I think that is Rick's special gift, and the main reason a book like this is worth reading. He describes how his faith connects with his life in such a distinctive way that you end up feeling like you have a new friend—or perhaps a new kind of friend who can help you figure out some God things without all that religious drama.

BART CAMPOLO
Speaker, writer and neighborhood minister

Only read one book a year? This is the one. Grew up in the church but have questions about living out your faith? This book is for you. Don't give a rip about Jesus? You'll especially enjoy this book . . . you'll have answers for your pesky Christian friends. Getting practical Christian living ideas from a surfer . . . sign me up! Count me stoked. Finally, a book I can read, understand and actually use. Rick, I love your sermons, and now your book.

GARY DIXON
Chairman of the Northwest Ministry Conference and consultant with David C. Cook

We all have different struggles, and we often have the wrong mindset or are too stubborn to change. As I read *Deep Like Me,* I was encouraged to rethink the way I approach God, people and life's circumstances. It encouraged me to seek the Lord on the different struggles in my life and how He truly wants me to live. Thanks for the hug, Rick! (:

BETHANY HAMILTON
Bestselling author of *Soul Surfer* and first-place winner of the Explorer Women's Division's, 2005 NSSA National Championship

At a time when many in the Church see people who fail as "expendable," Rick Bundschuh reminds us of the redemptive nature of God. His words inspired me, challenged me and, perhaps most importantly, included me in the ongoing narrative of grace as told through Jesus Christ. *Deep Like Me* is a must-read for those who have tried to walk on water only to find themselves at the bottom of the sea—yet still feel the call to get out of the boat!

CARL JONES
Modern-day leper, rescued soul, friend of Jesus and former youth pastor

Deep Like Me rang true to my real world and resonated with me. Each chapter was its own unique journey based on one of Rick's life experiences—like parables from his life that brought hope and help to my life. The different chapters spoke to me in different ways—some bringing wonder, others grace, others encouragement—but the one thing they all had in common was that I was glad I read each one.

TIC LONG
A guy, a dad, a husband, a friend and, among other things, executive director of Youth Specialties

Rick puts thoughts and observations into words in a way that I imagine I would, but I never do. His writing is insightful, witty, accessible and smart. In *Deep Like Me*, Rick has managed to include all of the observations I thought were mine alone—musings about the faith that I've never been brave enough to share with others. I must warn you, though, if you read this book, you may never participate in a prayer meeting or walk through a shopping mall the same way again. You might have to re-examine some of the assumptions we all make about Christianity as it is experienced today. And you just might discover a whole new joy, and irreverence, in the process.

KEN MCCOY
Founder of JumpStart Ministries

Rick Bundshuh is a consummate storyteller, but it's more than that: He tells stories that get under my skin, wiggle around and change me. I think it is his self-effacing approach, or his humor, or the unvarnished truth of his gentle-yet-in-your-face suggestions. Or it's all of those things.

MARK OESTREICHER
Author, speaker, consultant and coach

Deep Like Me is brilliant! When Rick Bundschuh writes, we all need to listen.

DR. DAVID OLSHINE
Director of Youth Ministries, Columbia International University

Deep Like Me resonated with me in much the same way as my own pastor, Rick Warren's, great writing and teaching does: it's completely authentic. It contains kernels of truth about everyday life and the Christian walk and presents it in a refreshing and inspired way. This series of short stories packs a powerful punch. This is truly Rick's masterpiece, and it will hit you like the crystal liquid purple-blue waves of Hawaii . . . so be prepared to dive in and "get wet."

DAVID PACK
"Purpose Driven" Grammy-winning singer, songwriter and record producer

If you're looking for a predictable, clichéd, "feeling-happy-about-how-nice-it-is-to-be-a-Christian" book, don't bother reading this one! When Rick talks about going deep, it's about struggling for breath, trying to figure out which way is up and living dangerously—all for the sake of seeing the beauty that is only available to those who are willing to go deep. This book expresses the thoughts and questions that most of us have when we try to live with integrity. You will be encouraged and challenged by *Deep Like Me*.

MARV PENNER
Chair of the Youth and Family Ministry department at Briercrest Graduate School

Christians and non-Christians alike should appreciate Rick's humor and down-to-earth style. *Deep Like Me* is honest, funny and to the point—but never preachy or overbearing. People who like Donald Miller will like this book. I did.

PIERCE PETTIS
Singer and songwriter

In *Deep Like Me*, Rick Bundschuh wraps the "everydayness" of life within the compelling and powerful love of God. Beautifully written and wonderfully entertaining, this book unveils God's purpose in transforming ordinary encounters into extraordinary lessons. It is engaging, familiar and affecting.

SHANE STANFORD
Pastor and author of *When God Disappears*

DEEP LIKE ME

rick bundschuh

DEEP LIKE ME

(OR ANOTHER FAILED ATTEMPT TO WALK ON WATER)

EXTREMELY PROFOUND THOUGHTS ON FAITH FROM A DISCIPLE IN OVER HIS HEAD

Gospel Light

From Gospel Light
Ventura, California, U.S.A.

Published by Regal
From Gospel Light
Ventura, California, U.S.A.
www.regalbooks.com
Printed in the U.S.A.

Library of Congress Cataloging-in-Publication Data
Bundschuh, Rick, 1951-
Deep like me (or another failed attempt to walk on water): Extremely profound thoughts on faith from a disciple in over his head / Rick Bundschuh.
p. cm.
ISBN 978-0-8307-4688-0 (trade paper)
1. Christian life. 2. Bundschuh, Rick, 1951- I. Title.
BV4501.3.B858 2009
248.4—dc22
2008044818

Rights for publishing this book outside the U.S.A. or in non-English languages are administered by Gospel Light Worldwide, an international not-for-profit ministry. For additional information, please visit www.glww.org, email info@glww.org, or write to Gospel Light Worldwide, 1957 Eastman Avenue, Ventura, CA 93003, U.S.A.

To order copies of this book and other Regal products in bulk quantities, please contact us at 1-800-446-7735.

*For Mike Wellman, long-time fellow explorer,
comrade and friend.*

CONTENTS

FOREWORD

In the author's own words, this is a book "designed to be an easy read with each chapter a musing of a different kind of Christianity."

In my pastoral ministry of more than 50 years, I have not known another person quite like Rick Bundschuh, nor have I read a book quite like this one. Rick served Christ with me as my youth director on the staff of Sierra Madre Congregational Church, in Southern California, back in the late seventies. As you read you will find that Rick covers much of the landscape of real life. At the same time, he faithfully responds to the biblical call to authentic Christian living. As I read chapter after chapter, the workings of his mind honestly amazed me. His musings are of a different kind, but his Christianity is biblically trustworthy.

As long as I have known this fellow pastor, who is also a gifted writer, I have always wondered at the way his mind works. Having finished reading this manuscript, I am still to a great degree amazed by his unique and refreshing perspective on people and life. This unlikely disciple, Rick Bundschuh, is alive in the pages of this book. As you read these chapters, you will surely get to know and experience this down-to-earth Christian who can juxtapose the realities of the human condition with a firm faith in the grace of God. I found my spirit rejoicing as he consistently seemed able to hear the best things about God from within the perplexing complexities of a fallen world. Because the writer consistently knows how to find his way back to God's mercy and grace, I believe you will find this book both realistic and redemptive!

I found the whole book most stimulating, but it was especially the chapter titled "On Being Wet" that said things to me I think need to be heard by the whole Family of God! So I say to you, read on; and to the author, thank you, my good brother Rick. Thank you for saying what I deeply feel when I am in my closest connection with God, but have never been able to express quite as effectively as this unlikely disciple.

Dick Anderson
Sierra Madre Congregational Church
Sierra Madre, California

ACKNOWLEDGMENTS

I am deeply indebted to the many named and unnamed individuals who have allowed me to weave their stories into these narratives. (You should be careful about what you share with authors; they are always taking notes for their next book.)

Please forgive me for any slight errors or exaggerations; I tried to get the facts down the best I could.

To my wife, Lauren, who patiently lets me run ideas past her but will probably only read any final draft of a book of mine posthumously, I owe gratitude for her love and encouragement.

Thanks also go to the congregation of wild characters who make up Kauai Christian Fellowship for the inspiration and fodder that weave in and out of these stories.

I owe a huge debt to all those men and women over the years whose influence and love have whacked away at my rough edges (a job not yet done) and helped shape me into a little better traveling companion. There are far too many of you to name, and of course if I did print your name you would expect a free book.

Finally, to the gang at Regal Books, especially Bill Greig Jr., Alex Field and Kim Bangs. I am greatly indebted to you for gambling on such an odd book. I hope we can sell enough so that you will be indebted to me.

INTRODUCTION

I am often uneasy being a Christian.

Some of that uneasiness comes because I am embarrassed by the myopic and clanging viewpoints adopted as eternal truth by some facets of Christianity. I cringe at the unvarnished ploys for money, power and prestige that drive a surprising number of leaders. I am extremely discomforted by those who have done spiritual plastic surgery on historic Christianity because they wanted to be trendy, and have ended up with a scary, unreal and silicone-filled configuration of the Christian faith.

I am uneasy with a whole lot of what is done and said in the name of Jesus.

But most of all, I am uneasy with me.

I find myself tottering around the edge of the cliff of commitment, encouraging others to take a plunge that I have been far too reluctant to take myself.

I am uneasy that after so many decades of being a Christian I still have so much pride, foolishness and lack of discipline hiding just under a well-ordered surface.

I have been asked to follow Jesus but I often find myself shuffling along behind Him at a distance, my mind being distracted and my journey being interrupted by other things.

I am an unlikely and somewhat reluctant disciple.

I am not a spiritual draftee or one who is a Christian because faith is a family legacy. I came to faith out of some crazy mix of my own free will, God's unstoppable magnetism, logical procession of common sense, well-modeled Christian example, clearly explained evangelism and some kind of deep inner call and response.

But it took awhile.

I am not the kind of personality that goes for the hard sell or jumps on a popular bandwagon just because it is popular. Before I was a reluctant disciple I was a reluctant convert.

At first, Christianity scared me because I feared it was insensible, unscientific, hysteria driven, ignorant and mostly mythical.

I think this fear is justified, because much of what is offered up as Christian is often flavored with those very things.

The thing that attracted me for a second look was that I kept running into intelligent, balanced, sensible, attractive and extremely witty people who took this faith seriously.

Still, it took awhile to feel as if my big questions had been answered and that there was enough evidence to warrant a step of faith. I circled the question of faith for over a year and a half, nudging closer and closer but still reluctant to step in.

Not all reasons for my hesitation were satisfied when I stumbled across the threshold into faith in Christ. I was, and remain, a believer with issues.

One of the interesting results of taking my sweet time to check out the Christian faith before signing up was that, unlike many who saw a good thing and rushed into it, I had a much better idea of what the next step would be. It would not be good enough to merely change signage from unbeliever to believer. I would have to become a disciple of Jesus as part of this journey.

I think Jesus was a strong proponent of careful reluctance over impetuousness. Remember that it was He who gave these little examples to those who were considering following Him: "Is there anyone here who, planning to build a new house, doesn't first sit down and figure the cost so you'll know if you can complete it? If you only get the foundation laid and then run out of money, you're going to look pretty foolish. Everyone passing by will poke fun at you: 'He started something he couldn't finish.' Or can you imagine a king going into battle against another king without first deciding whether it is possible with his ten thousand troops to face the twenty thousand troops of the other? And if he decides he can't, won't he send an emissary and work out a truce?" (Luke 14:28-36, *THE MESSAGE*).

After a lot of soul-searching, I decided that I might have what it takes to follow Jesus, to be His disciple. Being a disciple was not separate from knowing Christ; it was part of the whole package, and I knew it.

But in the back of my mind, I could hear the laughing. "He started something he couldn't finish! Ha! Ha! Ha! He has no idea what he is in for! Ha! Ha!"

To be quite frank, it is the fear of that taunt that has some-times been the spur to get up and keep the excursion going.

I went from reluctant and unlikely convert to reluctant disci-ple, but this time the focus of my reluctance had changed. Initially, I was reluctant about God. I wondered if all this stuff was worthy of such a bright young lad as myself. I questioned how He could be considered loving and still tolerate a world of starving children, brutal humans and natural disasters. I questioned His credentials, His identity and why the God of the Bible was, among all other contenders, the real McCoy.

After slipping across the line of faith, the focus of my reluc-tance changed. Now I was reluctant about myself. I started to see the impossibility of the journey, the staggering heights I would be asked to ascend and the distances that I would be asked to cover; and beside all of my outside bravado to the contrary, I wondered if I could really do this.

I think a lot of my co-travelers have the same hesitations. Of-ten they disguise it with an annoying gung-ho for Jesus, "I am invincible" kind of religious rhetoric. They feel compelled to dis-guise their own reluctance because they confuse honesty with lack of faith.

Yes, I know "I can do all things through Christ who strength-ens me," but when you are nudged off that path there is a lot of free falling and boulder clipping before God's safety line catches.

Part of the great irony of my journey is that I found myself as a pastor—first as an extension of a love for and natural disposi-tion to work with young people in youth ministry, and then kick-ing and screaming into birthing and shepherding an entire congregation. I never set out to be an officer, but it seems I had a battlefield commission.

I have often wondered about the sanity of putting a flawed, bat-tle scarred skeptic in such an honored position, but then I figured that the lunatics would rather have one of their own to lead them. And, if the Bible stories of all the unlikely knuckleheads appointed to take the responsibilities they were in no way prepared to handle are any indication, this kind of stuff seems to give God kicks.

To add unlikely probabilities to even more unlikely probabilities, I somehow found myself writing books that publishers wanted to print and thus came to uneasily wear the coveted mantle of "author" as well.

In spite of those undeserved honors, I am still first and foremost a follower of Jesus. And dragging the slowly shuffling herd of His unlikely disciples behind Him, Jesus takes us to breathtaking and dangerous places, with occasional visits to the infamous "peaceful still waters" sprinkled in. I have found my travels with Jesus to be an odd mix of joy, struggle, awe, confusion, serenity, faith, doubt, ease and hard work.

The following musings are notes and stories about that journey.

I have a strange feeling that I am not alone in the shuffle, and perhaps the thoughts of this oft-distracted fellow traveler might in some strange way encourage others who are just as loath to acknowledge how little real progress they have made toward being like Christ. Maybe by realizing our own stumbling and distractions, and knowing that we are not alone in our inconsistencies, it would encourage us to keep on plodding behind the Master.

Rick Bundschuh
Kauai, Hawaii

DEEP LIKE ME

1

SHUFFLING BEHIND JESUS

Some people have epiphanies—points in time when massive spiritual clarity and change flood their lives. They discover the meaning of the cross, take the offer of forgiveness and grace, stand in line to be a follower of Jesus, and allow Him permission to make new people out of them.

The vehicle God uses for these sudden leaps of understanding vary from individual to individual. For some an epiphany is a result of a church service or evangelical meeting; for some it came at the end of camp or retreat; for others the change was brought on through quiet discussion with a friend, the birth of a child, the death of a friend, the reading of an insightful book, a powerful movie or just a pile of alone time. And in spite of the devices some churches are married to, I don't think God is particular about the vehicle He uses.

Many Christian communities rely on creating events as an environment for these big life changes. We count up at the end of an event or service to see how many lives have taken a dramatic step, and we love to feature testimonials from people who have suddenly "seen the light." I am not against these kinds of gatherings or events, but they don't work for everyone the same way.

But some of us don't have too much in the way of show-stopping epiphanies. Our "Ah ha!" moments come in much less dramatic ways. Our moments of spiritual clarity are more like removing some smudge from the window of our understanding than a clicking on of a floodlight in a pitch-black room.

Rather than the inside-out, total conversion experience that typifies some people's encounters, our kind of rebirth in Christ comes in small bits and pieces. One day we wake up to realize that He pretty much has all the parts of us.

Even if we have had one or two powerful spiritual jolts, most of us don't continue our journey in faith by a continuing flow of exhilarating experiences. Those who try this just get nuttier and nuttier or they simply just wear out.

The vast majority of us just kind of ooze toward Jesus.

The progress of our faith may have some growth spurts, just like when our kids go to bed at night and wake up in the morning two inches taller and needing larger shoes. But most of our progress is subtle, slow and in increments almost too small to measure.

The development is better described as a journey, where change takes place along the way. It is where we build spiritual muscle and acclimate to the environment of the Kingdom.

What makes *this* journey unique is that we aren't in charge of choosing the path, we only have a vague idea of where we will end up (something about being Christlike as the final destination), and we are, sometimes anxiously, trying to figure out how to follow behind the Master for the whole trip.

I come to this journey unequipped. I quickly find the ground unfamiliar, the path far more narrow and difficult than I had imagined. I get tired of climbing so much. Jesus lets me stop, drink in the view and rest once in a while, but I prefer to camp instead.

Actually, I don't even want to camp. I want to park myself right here, cut down a few trees, clear a field and homestead. Then Jesus rousts me and beckons me to keep on going a bit "further up, further in."

I am a lousy traveling companion. I dawdle and get distracted easily with tidbits and trinkets along the trail. I look for short cuts and often venture down pointless bunny trails.

He leads; I shuffle.

While I mosey along the way, others who are going in both directions pass me. Some, who have a lot more discipline and endurance, move ahead of me, while others, who have given into the tempting pull of earthward gravity, are now taking a journey away from Jesus.

Those on their descent never make eye contact as they pass me.

Along the way one finds out some amazing things.

As we chance to slide over to the edge and see things a little closer to the vantage point God has, things seem clearer. The clarity causes us to cast off some old accepted wisdom and behavior. The view creates a whole new gist of reality.

Often God's way of doing things is a bit disconcerting and difficult to fathom. Seeing a few items from His perspective helps make sense out of what had, at one time, appeared senseless.

I would prefer that God worked in some sort of prescribed fashion. Get the code, punch the buttons and—*voilá!*—the door swings open for you. Indeed, to scan many of the book titles offered to the Christian public, this is exactly what we can achieve. We can drug-proof our kids, affair-proof our marriages, have financial peace, slim down forever and walk strong in faith every day of our lives.

Right.

Having read some of those kinds of books, I do acknowledge they have lots of good tips that are true in a general kind of way; but having spent a good number of years trying to drag my sorry soul behind Jesus, I have discovered some surprising things.

I've found that some believers, in spite of doing all the right things, still find difficulty and disappointment in the journey. They keep on going not because they hope that good things will sooner or later happen to them but because they believe that God Himself is good and that He loves them . . . in spite of what appears to be evidence to the contrary.

I found that some of the most popular worship songs and hymns that we sing were forged in a scorching fire of misery, depression and despair instead of bubbling out of some happy Christian place.

I found that some people who I thought were shallow were actually very deep, and some that I thought so wise were in reality shallow mimics.

I found that God seemed to take great pleasure in toppling my preconceived notions as fast as I could stack them up.

I found that you could know the Bible backwards and forwards and still act like a complete idiot.

I found grace and mercy in places I never expected to find them and condemnation and judgment in places where I expected to find grace and mercy.

I found believers who didn't really believe, and a few who claimed that they didn't believe to be far closer to believing than even they realized.

I found some with deep, heartfelt faith who had happy endings, and some with even deeper faith who experienced gut-wrenching and disastrous endings.

I found that there were people who concluded that my honest attempts to care about them were attempts to control them or harm them; and there were people who believed I loved and cared about them even though I treated them with mild indifference.

I found my journey behind Jesus not to be the easy, clear, orderly, linear little cruise I had imagined, but rather a tough, tangled, messy and sometimes confusing affair.

Please don't get me wrong, my faith is not shaken, it is just surprised. I continually have to readjust my thinking about things that I thought I had all figured out.

I am not suggesting that we can't rely on the promises in the Bible or that God can't be trusted; it is just that there is a lot of fine print written in these deals, and sometimes I am still startled at what I signed up for.

> *Calling the crowd to join his disciples, he said, "Anyone who intends to come with me has to let me lead. You're not in the driver's seat; I am. Don't run from suffering; embrace it. Follow me and I'll show you how. Self-help is no help at all. Self-sacrifice is the way, my way, to saving yourself, your true self. What good would it do to get everything you want and lose you, the real you? What could you ever trade your soul for?"*

> Mark 8:34-37, *THE MESSAGE*

> *Do you see what this means—all these pioneers who blazed the way, all these veterans cheering us on? It means we'd better get on with it. Strip down, start running—and never quit!*

*No extra spiritual fat, no parasitic sins. Keep your eyes on Jesus,
who both began and finished this race we're in. Study how he did it.
Because he never lost sight of where he was headed—that
exhilarating finish in and with God—he could put up with
anything along the way: Cross, shame, whatever. And now he's
there, in the place of honor, right alongside God. When you find
yourselves flagging in your faith, go over that story again, item
by item, that long litany of hostility he plowed through.
That will shoot adrenaline into your souls!*

Hebrews 12:1-3, *THE MESSAGE*

2

THE $3,000 HANDBAG

Last month I found myself wandering through a high-end mall. Normally, my forays into shopping malls are very simple. I hunt. I race in, bag the desired game and race out. No lingering at the food court, no pawing over sale items, no people watching or goodie browsing. Like most guys, I go to a store to buy something that I need and then go home and use it. (We men are simple creatures.)

But having time to kill that day I wandered in and out of shops. I spent time lusting for faster/newer electronics at the Apple Store; I went to see what cool useless toys there were to play with at Sharper Image; I bought a snack and even went in to check out the goods in stores that normally I never would have bothered to glance at.

Call me a Neanderthal, call me a Walmart refugee case; but I swear to you, I had no idea that stores in high-rent malls could exist selling only handbags or a small selection of shoes!

In my wanderings, I moseyed into a lush, well-appointed store that sold only a very limited selection of handbags. Each handbag had its own small platform and special lighting. Each wall had less than a dozen handbags, and every handbag was displayed as if it were the crown jewel.

The people working in the store were very nice, but they seemed to be eyeing me suspiciously. I tried to act casual, confident and nonchalant—a potential customer, not a time-killing looky-loo—as I wandered around viewing their very small sample of handbags and purses.

I suppose that people who go into stores like this one know better than to check the price tag. If you have to ask about price you are already out of your league and had better high tail it off to some place you can afford . . . like Sears. But, novice in the world of high fashion shopping that I am, I wandered over to a purse that I thought perchance my wife would find attractive and lifted the thing up.

The purse was a simple thing: leather strap, gold-toned snaps, durable cloth, leather exterior and markings of some kind.

There was no price tag.

By this time the saleslady had no doubt seen through my attempt at sophistication and she floated up behind me as I fumbled with the purse.

"Uh, er, there's no price tag on this," I stammered.

"There is," she assured me, and she unsnapped the purse and unfolded a small golden thread on which a small dainty price tag was attached. "This model," she said with the kind of pride that comes from knowing that there are actually models of handbags, "goes for $3,000."

I gasped—out loud. I didn't mean to. I mean, I expected the handbag to be a bit pricey, but THREE GRAND for a small sliver of cloth with a bit of animal hide and lacing?

"Dollars?" I mumbled stupidly. (As if they were pricing with pesos or monopoly money.) The saleslady politely nodded and then slowly moved back to her station. She obviously knew that I was a mere country hayseed who had stumbled wide-eyed and mouth agape into the big city. There would clearly be no sale from this customer.

I stood with the $3,000 purse in my unworthy hands and wondered exactly what it takes to make such a carrier of lipstick, keys and do-dads cost so much? My cover of debonair gentleman/metrosexual now blown, I decided at least to try to educate myself.

"Excuse me," I begged the clerk humbly. "But could you please explain to me what makes this purse so expensive?" (Could there be a hidden pocket with diamonds? Is this the purse that Joan of Arc carried with her to the stake? Come on—give me a good answer!)

"Oh, we have others here that are much more expensive than that," she replied, and then she went on a brief explanation about

Italian designers and Lamborghinis, craftsmanship, fine leather, and so on. But by then I was no longer paying much attention. My mind had taken its own journey—trying to come to grips with the idea that there are actually people paying $3,000 (or more!) for a simple handbag. And, apparently, there are enough of them to keep this store in business.

I gave the saleslady a weak "Thank you" at the end of her explanation and quickly slinked out of the store. I wandered around the rest of that afternoon with my thoughts on that $3,000 purse. Could I ever justify spending that kind of money on such an object—especially after traveling in third-world countries and seeing what even a few dollars could do to relieve hunger and suffering? No. I became convinced that nobody, or at least not those who consider themselves committed Christians, could justify a $3,000 purse when there is pain and suffering in the world!

I felt good and self-righteous about my decisive clarity.

Then a little thing in the back of my mind said, *What about a $1,000 purse? Naw,* I quickly countered in thought. *Can't justify that in light of a Christian's responsibility to those who "have not," and to Him who just might at the end of time say, "I was hungry and you bought a $1,000 purse instead!"*

Okay, said the inner voice, *would you ever consider buying a $500 purse for your wife? Hmm,* I thought, *this is getting a bit tougher.* IF it was the ONLY purse she would have, and IF the purse would last the next 10 years (presuming that normally a cheap purse breaks every year), then yes, at what would come to $50 a year, I could justify that on the basis of quality and use. But the little voice wasn't through and wasn't impressed with my logic.

Well, how about a $200 purse? Couldn't the third world use the $300 difference . . . and surely a $200 purse must be well constructed enough?

You can probably see where this goes.

By the time I was done thinking about purses and handbags, I had come to the conclusion that the only safe thing to do is buy a $5.95 canvas tote and give whatever else I might have spent to ease the suffering of the poor. But then, this is an easy issue for me since I don't carry a purse or buy them. Nor do I plan to. And if my wife wants a purse, she can spend what she wants on one—as long as it's not $3,000 (or $1,000 or even $500).

By this time my encounter with the expensive purse had opened up a can of little mind worms. I think I can get most of the Christian community to line up with me on the immorality of spending three grand on a purse. I probably could get a number of them to stay with me down to a thousand.

And this is good.

We Christians have to be able to say, "Enough is enough"—if only to ourselves. And I think we agree that there is something seriously wrong if a believer spends inordinate amounts of cash on things that don't really matter, even if that believer can afford doing so. Even if they are generous to the poor already, they could always be even more generous.

But preaching to the rich Christian guys, the lottery winners and those who have lots and lots of excess is easy. "Stay out of high-end purse shops," we can bellow to them. "You will have to answer for every dollar you waste!"

The real rub, at least to me, comes when I look at my own life. How much is enough? At what point have I gone from reasonable and responsible spending to waste so egregious that I might as well condemn others to hunger, poverty and misery? How much stuff in my garage was bought on whim? How many "guy toys" clutter my closet? Will I have to answer for each and every one of them? Will I be called to account for every buck spent on stupid stuff such as trinkets and snacks I didn't need? I don't like asking myself the questions raised by the $3,000 purse. And I don't pretend I have any "right" answers. In fact, this is so uncomfortable that I'm tempted to not think about it at all—or to pull the blanket of grace up over my troubled conscience. But I don't think I have that option. Having that conversation with myself is very important, even if I don't like the conclusions I reach.

Then those "sheep" are going to say, "Master, what are you talking about? When did we ever see you hungry and feed you, thirsty and give you a drink?" Then the King will say,

*"I'm telling the solemn truth: Whenever you did one of these
things to someone overlooked or ignored, that was me—
you did it to me."*

Matthew 25:37,40, *THE MESSAGE*

*The only additional thing they asked was that we remember the
poor, and I was already eager to do that.*

Galatians 2:10, *THE MESSAGE*

3

ON BEING WET

"I'm looking for something deeper," she grumbled to me.

As one who enjoyed the particular Bible study that the woman was commenting on, I felt a bit conflicted. Part of me wanted to jump to the defense and blurt out, "Who in the heck do you think you are? This is good, solid stuff that may be familiar to some but is truly lived by few (especially you, you pompous airbag!)."

The other part of me was wondering if I were such a simpleton that I was settling for pabulum when there was a rich meaty world of cool spiritual ideas waiting for me to discover them.

So I just mumbled something incoherent in response.

She shook her head and that was the last I saw of her.

Presumably, she found the mother lode of spiritual depth that had eluded her with us.

Over the years that I have been on the journey, there were times when I found myself trying to become spiritually deep by filling my head with all kinds of theological jargon, or trying to work out one system of God-think or another. The often unintended result was that I tended to become brittle, indecipherable to the average Joe, condescending to the unwashed masses, argumentative . . . and very proud of it.

I found myself creating strong positions on what in reality was pretty thin biblical ice. I sensed the fragility, but getting deeper and getting meatier in my mind demanded that I stake myself out in this bleak landscape. Besides, I had the company of other similarly minded deep thinkers.

Together we scoffed at those in the shallows of the Christian experience. We chuckled at those whose faith was elementary and simple. We rolled our eyes at those who, like a parrot, used words they couldn't even define simply because it was the Christian-speak they had picked up along the way.

We thought being "deep" was the goal that every Christian ought to aspire to and were constantly frustrated by those who wouldn't be baited to join us in the deep end of Christian thinking.

But, as has happened to me on numerous other occasions in my clumsy trek behind Jesus, it turned out that I was thinking wrongly.

Not only was I wrong, but I was also screwy, Pharisaical and full of myself.

Now please don't misunderstand. I think Christianity is a faith of tremendous depths to plumb and is full of intellectual challenges for those to whom God has given the gift and ability. Staying spiritually infantile is not a good thing. Growth in our intelligence ought to develop along with growth in our character, growth in our spirit and growth in our human connections as we mature in our relationship with Christ.

The problem is that we are measuring what really matters by the wrong standard. We think that getting into complex theological knots or having some kind of inside track (often noted by special words such as "anointed" or "powerful") is a sign of Christian brilliance that we ought to aspire to.

I have come to believe that those things can often get in the way of what *really* matters to God.

Perhaps I can use a word picture to explain what I think really matters.

Let's imagine that Christianity is like a huge swimming pool.

This pool has a shallow end with broad steps gently leading into the water. It is a perfect place for those who are fearful of water or for young ones and the uninitiated to become acquainted with this new discovery and its possibilities. It is a place to experience the giddy joy of releasing our land-bound bodies to an aqua world.

This pool gently slopes down toward a very deep end.

The depth at the opposite end of the pool is so great that the water is dark blue and the bottom is invisible. Some have tried to discover the end of the fathoms below them, but they have all failed.

Between these two extremes is a vast length of pool where one can move freely from waist-deep to barely touching on tiptoes.

Some will spend most of their time here; some will find themselves dog paddling over the deep end of the pool for a while but going back to rest where they can touch bottom; and some will never leave where they can firmly feel the bottom. Many will simply twirl in the shallows, splashing happily.

And it doesn't matter.

I believe that God does not care all that much if we get deep or shallow in the great pool that is Christianity. What He does care about is that we *get wet*.

One can be no less wet rolling about on the entry steps as someone who is struggling in the deep end.

Wetness can occur when you hear a child sing, "Jesus loves me, this I know . . ." as well as when reading a chunk of the writings of Augustine.

Wetness can occur among out-of-tune guitars, less than on-pitch voices and misspelled lyrics projected on a screen, as well as during a finely crafted set by a renowned worship leader.

Wetness can take place during a simple reciting of stuff we already know as well as during a presentation where the speaker is skilled and profound.

Wetness can (and often does) take place outside the walls of a church building and even once in a while within them.

What God wants is to envelop us with Himself, with His love, His mercy, His fragrant grace, His saturating joy.

Depth is not a requirement for this kind of wetness.

The wonder of this means that a novice, a child or a gangly teenager may be enjoying the surrounding presence of God far more than those of us who are looking for a Bible study with depth or a preacher who gives us the "meat of the Word."

Perhaps the deep end of our Christian experience isn't one that we ought to seek but something that we drift into as we simply enjoy splashing in the shallows.

All I know is that for myself, I care much more about being wet than being deep. I am much happier enjoying God's presence than being right or theologically brilliant.

Blessed are those who have learned to acclaim you,
who walk in the light of your presence, O LORD.

Psalm 89:15, *NIV*

You have made known to me the path of life; you will fill me with
joy in your presence, with eternal pleasures at your right hand.

Psalm 16:11, *NIV*

4

THE SACRIFICIAL LAMB

"Why me?"

"What did I do to deserve this?"

"It's not fair."

Kids say these things out loud. Adults usually just think them. We think these thoughts for the kind of small things in life: when the coveted job goes to someone else who is less industrious and qualified; when we, honest in doing our taxes, get audited; when the guy next door gets another shiny new car just around the time our beater throws a timing chain.

But most of all we think these things when disaster looms on the horizon. When our spirit is about to take a licking. When hope evaporates and specters of danger and destruction cloud around us.

We wonder about God. We develop serious questions about His love, His plan for us, His protection and His wisdom.

We implore the heavens for a word of comfort or sensible explanation; yet, other than the echo of our own words, there is nothing but silence.

In our worst moments, we feel God has abandoned us, He has tricked us and our heart becomes utterly hopeless.

I remember seeing a flash of that feeling of hopeless abandonment in the eyes of my second oldest son. It was only for a moment, but it was clear and panic filled. Under normal circumstances I would have dealt with it, but to be honest, at the time I was having too much fun.

Oh, but before branding me a monster or calling child protective services, hear the whole story.

Being a new fifth grader in a new school and a new place is a drag. Unknown and friendless, a kid has to haul his carcass across the campus while trying to avoid those who would poke at him experimentally, like a toad on the road, to see what it will take to get him to jump.

My son Justin entered a brand-new grade school here in Hawaii when he was in fifth grade. Fresh from the mainland, he didn't know a soul. He was ripe to be tested by the junior gangs, cliques and alpha males of the school. It was, and even now is, the natural order of things.

I was taking the trashcans out to the curb when the school bus passed at the end of the block. School was out and kids were coming home.

As I lugged a second trashcan to the curb, I noticed Justin racing around the corner from the bus stop.

I thought nothing of it. When I was a kid, I would sometimes sprint toward home when I had a full bladder or an extra dose of sugar energy to burn off.

Then I saw four other kids running around the corner as well.

Justin was barreling up the block at full speed; the other boys were doing their best to close in on his heels. I stood there, full trash container in hand, watching the chase.

Justin passed me without saying a word and made a hard left up the driveway toward the safety of the back door.

The gang of four, who had almost caught up to him, screeched to a halt within a foot of me, suddenly realizing that their mark had made it home to his lair and, even worse, Papa bear was standing there holding a trash can.

Now what went on in my mind took place in microseconds but it was a whole reasoned-out scenario and plan.

My boy was safe, but only for the moment. These same boys would be on his trail at another place or time.

Plus, I didn't have all the facts. Perhaps my son did something to really tick off these guys, such as giving one of their little brothers a swirly or something. (Swirl-y: The act of putting someone into the toilet bowl head first and then flushing.)

At any rate, I didn't want to jump to conclusions and start chewing out this posse without all the evidence. Besides, like any father worth his salt, I was trying to teach my son to fight his own battles.

The solution came in a flash.

"Look!" I said to the waffling boys, "I don't know what my kid did that made four of you want to chase him down, but I tell you what, we can solve it here and now . . . but not four on one . . . one to one."

The boys blinked and looked at each other as I called Justin back and then continued speaking.

"You see, I have a couple pair of boxing gloves inside. I'll get them and we can go out on the lawn and settle this man to man, one on one. I'll be the ref to make sure that nobody gets hurt too badly."

Justin's eyes bugged out of his head.

His own father had just offered to make him a sacrificial lamb. And he would have to take on four challengers!

Ah, but I already knew better. I've been around for a while and I knew that if it took four guys to handle one guy, there is already a strong whiff of cowardice in the air.

"Well!" I said in a decisive tone, "Who wants to go first?"

Eyes darted to view shoes. Hemming and hawing commenced, fidgeting erupted.

I knew there would be no takers.

The wheels were turning in their little fifth-grade minds.

If the father is anxious to have his son fight us . . . that must mean the kid is a pro boxer and we are going to get our clocks cleaned, one by one, they were reasoning to themselves.

Sensing their cowardice, I prodded them on. "So, you guys wanted to fight, here's your opportunity! Which of you brave guys is going to step up first?"

More shrinkage.

Then I went for the jugular.

"Oh, I see how it is! You are big and brave when it is four on one, but you are a bunch of sissies when you've gotta stand up on your own!"

Now I was on fire. I delivered the final blow to their cocky little egos with manly and theatrical disdain, spitting out my lines with flourishes. "You bunch of pantywaists, you pathetic little cowards! Get the heck outta here and don't let me catch you bugging my kid again or I'll give him permission to wipe the floor with you!"

The crew slinked away, tails tucked up tightly as they headed for home, thankful that they did not have to have a one-to-one face-off with the skinny little new kid who would kick their butts.

I watched them silently creep off and then turned to my son, smiled and wiped my hands in mock glee.

He still couldn't believe I would offer him up to the slaughter.

"Aww," I said reassuringly, "I KNEW they were cowards and would never take me up on the offer!"

I don't know if he bought it or thought he just got off lucky that afternoon. But obviously the word got out in "kiddom," and not one little punk bully tried to tempt fate with the newcomer for the rest of the year.

When I retell this story, most dads think the way I handled the situation was pretty cool and most moms want me to stay away from their children . . . forever.

But other than basic child rearing drama, there is a lesson to be learned here.

You see, God is not above putting you or me in very awkward, potentially disastrous situations that seem to be, from our earth-bound vantage point, the antithesis of what a loving heavenly Father would do.

My journey has produced a quiver of these faith-shaking, gut-twisting, seemingly spiritually orphaned moments.

Oh, but His wisdom, His insight and His judgments are so much greater than ours, and the outcome so much clearer to Him!

Just ask Joseph, who must have thought his world had come to an end when God allowed him to be victimized by his brothers, set up by his master's wife and tossed into jail.

Or Gideon, as he was, at God's request, dismissing men from his army to go home on the eve of a huge battle.

Or Moses, Abraham and hosts of others.

God was up to something much bigger than they realized.

Those times when the task seems impossible, when the burden is overwhelming and the odds are against you may just be the time when God has everything totally in control.

It is just not convenient for Him to let you in on it.

*GOD, investigate my life; get all the facts firsthand.
I'm an open book to you; even from a distance, you know
what I'm thinking. You know when I leave and when I get back;
I'm never out of your sight. You know everything I'm going to
say before I start the first sentence. I look behind me and you're
there, then up ahead and you're there, too—your reassuring
presence, coming and going. This is too much, too wonderful—
I can't take it all in!*

Psalm 139:1-6, *THE MESSAGE*

*"For I know the plans I have for you," declares the
LORD, "plans to prosper you and not to harm you,
plans to give you hope and a future."*

Jeremiah 29:11, *NIV*

5

EVERY TUESDAY

I have a confession to make. I really struggle with prayer, or at least prayer in the sense that seems to be practiced by most Christians.

This is not a new problem; it has plagued me from the very start of my journey with Christ. And I know that putting this confession in print puts my standing for sainthood in serious jeopardy.

Perhaps this admission is like talking about a secret that is too fearful to blurt out and still keep your spiritual aura intact. Yet, possibly for a few other souls, it could even be a burst of relief. "Thank God! I am not alone in this dilemma."

It's not like I don't pray. In fact, I used to pray sometimes before I was a Christian—they were let's-keep-things-cool prayers like "Please, God, don't let my mom find out," or big-vow emergency prayers like "If you don't let this cop notice, I promise I will never do it again!" But of course like most prayers of this nature, they were simply talismans to grab in desperation, not a serious attempt to commune with the Almighty; unless, of course, He was handing out cash or free Super Bowl tickets.

After I became a Christian I came to realize that people got really serious about prayer. They didn't just pray during emergencies, they prayed all the time. They had prayer before everything and at the end of everything. They had special meetings set aside for nothing else but prayer. Some people I met even made lists of things to pray for each day and got up before dawn to start down the list.

And it is obvious that some revel in prayer or, in particular, prayer meetings.

Like the guy who can't shut up once he gets into a conversation, a number of people I met would start to talk to God out loud and then go on and on and on and on and on, leaving others to wonder if they should match, raise or fold when it came their turn to pray.

If a nice long prayer time is a meal to some people, then I am a snacker.

I seem to have acute prayer attention deficit. A little bit and I'm done. A nibble and I've had all I can stomach. At one time during my journey this fact haunted me with shame, but I've worked through it.

Recently, we had a community-wide prayer meeting. It was made up of folks from many churches; as a church leader, I was urged to go. It was supposed to last for two hours, which is about an hour and 56 minutes longer than I can concentrate.

The truth be told, I can't stand prayer meetings that last much over four minutes. After that, try as hard as I can, my focus drifts. I start to nod off and feel terribly guilty that I can't hang in there.

If I had lived a couple thousand years ago, I have no doubt that I would have been one of the disciples curled in a ball and snoring away in Gethsemane only to awaken to the withering reproof of Jesus.

I don't always fall asleep, but very often my mind drifts away.

Believe me, I try very, very hard to keep my thoughts focused on what the other person is praying for or about, but to no avail. My ADD brain turns and hops down just about any bunny trail of thought that comes along.

And if somebody gets the bright idea to hold hands while praying, all I can think about is the odd reality of hanging on to the sweaty mitt of somebody I barely know and how awkward I feel, especially if the person gives me the little hand squeeze at the end of the prayer. (Why do people do that anyhow?)

If I manage to stay awake or keep my mind from wandering, I may start hearing the . . . uh, um "peculiarities" of how the others who are praying go about addressing the Almighty.

I never know if I will find myself suppressing a giggle at the guy who, with great fervor, drops God's title in at every single hesitation point in his monologue: "Oh, Lord, we come to you tonight, Lord, to ask you, Lord, to please do your will, Lord, and to give us the strength, Lord, to do what you ask, Lord . . ."

I imagine what it would be like to have my wife make a request of me using the same verbiage: "Oh Rick, if you don't mind, Rick, could you, Rick, please fill my car with gas, Rick, because you, Rick, know how much I hate doing it, Rick!" Which of course makes me snicker even more because I know how annoying it sounds, and I can imagine God rolling His eyes and muttering a line that could come directly from an old *Monty Python* movie.

I begin to get irritated that many people pray much differently than they speak. A few even pray in Elizabethan English.

Some people get really into it, almost putting on a show, as if God will somehow work quicker, safer and more effectively with a bit of theatrics thrown in. Then I feel bad that I am being judgmental.

Sometimes I wonder if I also sound like a dork when I pray and then I feel stupid for wondering, because I am not praying to other people but to God.

I think.

Or if during some community prayer time, if others have already used up everything I can think of to pray about, I start to contemplate if I need to pray out loud at all. I wonder that if I don't say anything, will the prayer meeting hit a pause button (especially if the prayer seems to be going around in a circle).

My struggle with prayer is not merely in a group setting.

If I try to pray in the closet, I end up rearranging the shoes.

If I try to pray at the beach, I get distracted by every good wave, every sun goddess, every odd-looking person with more hair on his back than on his head, or every "why did you think it was a good idea to stuff that much flesh into a little bathing suit" case that strolls by.

Don't get me wrong. I can pray. Just not for very long.

To add to all of this, there is the mystery of prayer.

I know prayer works, I just don't know *how* it works, *when* it works or in *what manner* it works. I mean, the results are not predictable, even for the prayer warriors. It is not like a faucet where you move the handle, and every time you do, water pours forth, or a car where you turn the key and feel the engine roar.

You pray, maybe feel a little better and then you wait around to see what happens. Prayer seems to be more of a Crock-Pot than microwave in terms of results.

Throughout history people have sensed this mystery and have sometimes added strange things into their prayer life to get to the front of the request line: whacking themselves with little whips, crawling up chapel steps on their knees, starving themselves, and the like.

I understand their frustration, because prayer is so unlike the mechanical, put-the-coin-in-the-slot-and-get-instant-results world that it sometimes makes you want to scratch your head and wonder if prayer does any good at all.

But we good Christians don't ever wonder that out loud, for that would be a symptom of lack of faith, and we know that any prayers floating out there are sure to go in the tank if we have lack of faith.

Mix this in with God's unfathomable time table and the fact that some prayers may very well be answered by what you don't see happen instead of what you do see happen or by the answers "No!" or "Maybe!" and the whole thing gets pretty confusing for the average rank-and-file pray-er.

Yet, as difficult as prayer has been for me, there are bright spots.

The first was when I came to the conclusion that just because I couldn't handle long prayer sessions or stay focused, it didn't mean that I could not be a praying type of guy. I began to enjoy blurting out little itty-bitty prayers as they came to mind. They don't amount to much at the moment, but in the course of a day they become a long, running conversation with God.

I decided to avoid long prayer meetings or bail on them quickly. I try not to hold hands, but if I am trapped, I just start telling God how much I hate to be standing there holding hands with a woman other than my wife who smells of too much perfume . . . or even worse, some equally nervous guy. It may not be the reason we are gathered in prayer, but at least I am praying.

And I believe there is precedent for these grumbling type of prayers found all over the psalms.

In spite of a lifetime difficulty fitting into the current Christian rhythm of prayer, I occasionally get inspired to pray in ways that I once avoided.

Recently, a distant friend helped and humbled me in this regard.

I bumped into Marv Penner at a Christian event. Over the decades, we have seen each other at youth worker conventions or conferences once every year or two. Mostly we just make small talk for a minute and then run off.

Marv, who has gone from being a youth worker schmuck to being a professor at Briercrest Theological Seminary, was sitting at a table shooting the breeze with some other guys as I stumbled past. He acknowledged me with a wave and two words: "Every Tuesday!"

Nobody at the table knew what he was talking about. But I did.

You see, several decades ago, I was going through a real rough patch in life. Even though I didn't know Marv very well, he let me bleed on him. When our talk was done, he promised to pray for me every week.

And he has done so for 20 years or more, *every Tuesday*.

I marveled at the commitment of a man who is really not much more than an acquaintance. I was humbled that his lips had presented my name to the Almighty every Tuesday . . . and of course, I had *not* prayed for him at all during those years.

I began to wonder if all the blessings, opportunities and small miracles that have happily cluttered my life during the last 20-something years might be linked in some strange and mysterious way not to anything I have done or to any wise choices on my part, but to the fact that someone with a lot of other concerns and people in his life has been praying for me every Tuesday.

The Holy Spirit began to stir the prayer pot inside of me. If Marv could remember me every Tuesday, maybe I could get a few guys and pray for them by remembering what day it was. I would try to mix in both good friends and mere acquaintances. I would try to be as faithful to remember these people each week as Marv has been in praying for me.

Being as prayer disadvantaged as I am, I decided to start by praying for guys whose first or last names have the same letter as the day of the week. So now Mark and McCoy share Monday. Tom and Thompson get Tuesday. I have even expanded out of the alphabet to add John into Wednesday.

It feels good to pray for these people. The prayers are short and usually unspecific. And I have no idea what cosmic results, if any, they are having. But I look forward to the day when I can point to one of these friends or acquaintances with a smile and say, "Every Tuesday!" and know they will sense the presence of God working in their lives.

> *Be especially careful when you are trying to be good so that you don't make a performance out of it. It might be good theater, but the God who made you won't be applauding. When you do something for someone else, don't call attention to yourself. You've seen them in action, I'm sure—"playactors" I call them— treating prayer meeting and street corner alike as a stage, acting compassionate as long as someone is watching, playing to the crowds. They get applause, true, but that's all they get. When you help someone out, don't think about how it looks. Just do it—quietly and unobtrusively. That is the way your God, who conceived you in love, working behind the scenes, helps you out. And when you come before God, don't turn that into a theatrical production either. All these people making a regular show out of their prayers, hoping for stardom! Do you think God sits in a box seat? Here's what I want you to do: Find a quiet, secluded place so you won't be tempted to role-play before God. Just be there as simply and honestly as you can manage. The focus will shift from you to God, and you will begin to sense his grace. The world is full of so-called prayer warriors who are prayer-ignorant. They're full of formulas and programs and advice, peddling techniques for getting what you want from God. Don't fall for that nonsense. This is your Father you are dealing with, and he knows better than you what you need.*

Matthew 6:1-8, *THE MESSAGE*

6

THE LAUGHING BOX

I don't think it is any secret that for a good while now, we believers have had a problem keeping our most intimate relationships together; in particular, marriage.

People who claim Christianity as their faith divorce at the same statistical rate (and some suggest at an even greater rate) as professed unbelievers.

The resulting fallout has church staff scrambling to figure out how to deal with the divisions in their midst and the hoards of innocent family members and bystanders who take shrapnel when a marriage explodes.

This phenomenon, besides being shameful, is also very baffling. Explanations abound.

Some suggest that the faith of most who call themselves Christian is merely a thin spiritual icing on an otherwise dark and devious cake of personal secularism. Their obvious lack of commitment to the known will of God shows up in their utter disregard for anything that inconveniences them from doing whatever they really feel like doing.

Others fault the cultural environment that assumes monogamy, commitment and the basic notion of an intact family unit are ghosts of bygone eras and are not realistic burdens to be placed on such enlightened people as ourselves.

Still others put the finger on our sin nature as the culprit and make the point that many humans have historically been failures at relationships.

Then there is the "blame the church" crew who insist that if we were practicing church discipline the way we should, or doing a better job of teaching the Bible, a lot of believers would think twice about breaking their vows and running off to join another fellowship.

All the while, unbelievers snicker and take pleasure in the fact that the holier-than-thou crowd is all boast and bluster but no substance when it comes to the actual running of their lives.

To be honest, I wish I knew what the real reason is; perhaps it is all of the above, none of these explanations or some kind of mix of a few of them.

What I do know is that at the most basic level of human relationships there is something so fundamental and foundational that without it only misery is guaranteed. Without it no marriage, friendship or any other kind of bond is possible for long.

That thing is the ability to forgive.

Hang around with people for any length of time and you will get elbowed by a careless word, unkind deed or ungracious action. And the closer you are to someone, the more likely you are to get frequently whacked.

I think it is safe to say that most of the slights, hurts and disappointments we experience from others can be attributed to misunderstandings, misinterpretations, miscommunications, weariness, clumsiness, stress or other factors. The offense is many times accidental or impulsive instead of intentional.

This may not make the hurt any less painful, but it is much easier to forgive if we know that in his or her heart of hearts, this person does not wish us any harm.

But then there are those other situations where the hurt was aimed, intentional and well designed. Betrayal, deception, abuse, rage and degradation are the currency that will now be traded in place of love and caring.

The absence of deep hurts does not mean that a relationship will stay afloat. Huge violations are gashes in the hull of a marriage, but many couples are dragged to the bottom by the accumulation of small unforgiven hurts that are stowed away in the hold of the heart until they finally scuttle the relationship.

It is amazing how many of us who understand the depth of forgiveness offered to us for our sins are so intent on storing up the memory of wrongs done to us, as if it gives us some kind of wicked power over those who have offended us, or—heaven forbid—a perverse pleasure in having a reason to be angry or seek vengeance.

Frederick Buechner wisely commented on this twisted and ultimately self-destructive tendency shared among mortals:

> Of the Seven Deadly Sins, anger is possibly the most fun. To lick your wounds, to smack your lips over grievances long past, to roll over your tongue the prospect of bitter confrontations still to come, to savor to the last toothsome morsel both the pain you are given and the pain you are giving back—in many ways it is a feast fit for a king. The chief drawback is that what you are wolfing down is yourself. The skeleton at the feast is you.[1]

The secret to forgiveness seems to be to keep short accounts or, as the apostle Paul put it, not letting the sun go down on your anger (see Eph. 4:26).

Combine that with a healthy awareness of our own flailing elbows, and the offense dissolves like a lump of salt tossed in water.

This, like many other things we do, is not something that comes naturally but is a spiritual habit we work on and try to perfect. And it is best if it is practiced early in our walk of faith.

My friend Richard and his wife, Lorraine, have been married a long time and still sparkle with affection for each other. One night someone asked them their "secret."

A consummate joker, Richard wisecracked a reply, but when he was pressed again for a serious explanation of how someone could have a marriage that after many decades still shimmered with closeness and love, he smiled and said, "You have to get a laughing box!"

Lorraine giggled and said, "You can't just say that, now you have to tell them the whole story."

It seems that when Richard and Lorraine were in their early years of marriage, the adjustment from "me" to "us" was not always easy for Richard. This became especially true when Lorraine became pregnant with their first child and she lost the energy for late nights and some of the appetite for the spontaneity that had typified their lives as young adults.

And so it was that Richard ended up playing cards with his buddies and losing all sense of time while Lorraine waited for him to come home for dinner.

By the time Richard realized that he had blown it, Lorraine was in bed, steaming in anger, and had locked Richard out of the house.

For his part, Richard decided against a phone call or a race home, opting to stay with his pals for a few more hours and then slip home after Lorraine was sound asleep.

When Richard got home he found that he had been locked out in the cold and that Lorraine had even taken the time to latch down every window.

Uh oh, I'm in deep trouble now, Richard said to himself.

Finally, Richard found a small window he could jimmy open, and he slithered in and silently crept up to the bedroom.

It was very late, and Richard was as quiet as possible slipping into bed, but he knew instinctively that Lorraine was awake . . . and giving him the silent treatment.

Often for a man, the silent treatment is more torturous than anger or tears. The latter lances the boil; the silent treatment sustains it, often for days and sometimes even weeks.

Richard laid his head on the pillow. He knew he had screwed up and that any excuses he could come up with would come off lame. Apologies, too, wouldn't work at this stage in the quiet conflict.

He reached over to the bed stand and grabbed a little black box. It was a goofy battery-run object he had found at a novelty store. It had one button and a small speaker built inside; it was a laughing box.

In the late night darkness, with the chill of hurt feelings lowering the room temperature to near zero, Richard pressed the button on the laughing box.

The mechanically recorded human laugh burst into the silence with it's unspoken, attached message.

"Ha! Ha! Ha!" *I am such an idiot!*

"Hee, Hee, Hee!" *You were right to lock me out!*

"Ho, Ho, Ho." *Come on; please forgive me.*

Lorraine lay in the darkness, curled in a fetal position, back turned toward Richard.

Stupid laughing box, she thought. *Just like Richard to do this; he is a real character.*

Against her own better judgment she smiled.

The laughing box continued to chortle in the dark.

Other husbands would be groveling, begging for forgiveness, she thought to herself, *but I had to marry a guy who would tell me he is sorry by pressing a button on a laughing box in the middle of the night.*

And then she begins, in spite of herself, to laugh.

At first she tried to smother the laugh in the pillow, but it slipped out and she turned to look at Richard who was sitting up in bed, holding the laughing box and smiling his cat-that-ate-the-canary grin.

Lorraine hit him with her pillow, and in the darkness, they out-laughed the laughing box.

Quick forgiveness and, if necessary, a laughing box, may not solve all the woes plaguing our relationships, but it may be a good place to start.

"In your anger do not sin": Do not let the sun go down while you are still angry, and do not give the devil a foothold.

Ephesians 4:26-27, *NIV*

A man's wisdom gives him patience; it is to his glory to overlook an offense.

Proverbs 19:11, *NIV*

This is how I want you to conduct yourself in these matters. If you enter your place of worship and, about to make an offering, you suddenly remember a grudge a friend has against you, abandon your offering, leave immediately, go to this friend and make things right. Then and only then, come back and work things out with God.

Matthew 5:23-24, *THE MESSAGE*

Note
1. Frederick Buechner, *Wishful Thinking* (San Francisco: HarperOne, 1973).

7

LUIS'S TRUCK

I came of age during a brief moment of utopian madness. A lot of that utopian thinking rubbed off on me and I have had to work hard to become cynical. I have managed to be mostly cynical now, but every once in a while a little weed of utopianism escapes through some crack and begs to be left alone to turn into a tree.

Sometimes, against the advice of friends and colleagues, I let the thing grow. It may be some sort of residue from my past or simply a knee-jerk sympathy for lost causes. But often my family and friends have patronized me when I have an idealistic moment. After all, I am a survivor of the '60s.

The war was raging in Vietnam, civil rights had been guaranteed by the courts, and kids were busy casting off the culture of their parents. In the middle of this confusion a bunch of college kids without underwear or makeup decided to experiment with a strange kind of alternative lifestyle that, at it's inception, was not based exclusively on sex, drugs or rock 'n' roll, but on the naïve notion that human beings, with a bit of encouragement, would much rather be rolling in the daisies than pushing them up through war and violence. In a short time, someone labeled them "hippies."

Nobody, guys or girls, shaved anything or cut their hair. They went for lots of beads and homemade clothes spun of cotton or hemp, as well as thrift store castoffs. They had huge tribal picnics called "love-ins."

I am actually one of the few people I know who went to a love-in . . . and can remember it. I was just a kid at the time—a lanky, always hungry, young surfer with broad, tanned shoulders and uncontrolled sun-bleached hair.

The hippies were having their love-in at a beach park near where I lived. They were young, beaded, colorful and smelled oddly earthy. They had a cool little band set up and a ton of food laid out on the kind of neat-looking bedspreads that are made in India.

I rode up on my bike, astonished to see the cosmic circus had come to my hometown.

The people were kind to me. They invited me to sit down with them and have something to eat. I was shocked. As a young junior high boy, I was used to being shooed off or ignored by older people, not invited to a picnic.

Contrary to popular myth, nobody gave me "loaded" brownies or offered me drugs of any kind. They just shared their food, their music and a space on their bedspread.

Impressionable, and a sucker for anyone who gave me food with no strings attached, I thought their message of love and peace might actually have a chance.

By the end of the '60s it had all gone sour.

But some of the hippie crew had become Christians and were attempting to keep the love-in vibe alive by setting up Christian communes where believers could live out the lifestyle of a believer unfettered by private ownership of just about anything. (I think they got to keep their own toothbrushes.)

I went to visit a friend who had joined one of these communes.

They were a pretty proud bunch. They were proud that they had been courageous enough to live as they imagined the early believers lived during the opening salvos of the church. They were proud to be faithful to the first and purest instinct of those believers.

My friend made it a point to show me their prooftext for communal living, from Acts 2. Actually, he did more than show it to me; he rubbed my nose in it and suggested that if I really wanted to experience obedience to God, I needed to move in with them and sign my car over to the leading elder or "prophet" of the group.

I managed to escape immediate recruitment; but as I drove home, a wave of confusion washed over me. Were these folks really the faithful remnant, and the rest of us with cars in our name, private apartments and our own favorite coffee mug really missing the spiritual boat?

There *was* something idealistically inviting about the idea of having everything in common, especially for a young man who had not lived long enough for all things utopian to be rinsed out of him by the sad cynicism of everyday life. The loose grip on stuff of this world seemed to go right along with the teachings of Jesus I had tried to follow. But there was also something that didn't seem right about the whole situation—something that seemed to lurk under the surface that I could only sense but not quite see.

So I never went back.

Instead, I got more stuff that was *mine*.

And to confirm my hesitation, the commune soon turned cultish and then blew apart. The head elder/cult leader now had lots of cars and other people's stuff that he was now the legal owner of.

I understand that some of the young people involved were so discouraged by the collapse of the commune and resultant bickering, backstabbing and all-around nasty behavior that they walked away from Jesus as well.

Many decades later, I have lots of stuff that I call mine, so much so that unlike those carefree young years, I can no longer haul all of it around in a duffle bag. No, I need a moving van or a fleet of trucks.

We bought a house and filled it with stuff. Every year for over a decade we brought in way more stuff than we tossed out.

And then we decided to move. Not far, mind you, just a few miles away—too close to hire a moving van but close enough to get the job done with a few shuttles in a truck.

The problem was that I didn't own a truck.

But I knew a guy in our church who had a truck, which he would often lend to people who needed it. His name was Luis.

Luis had bought the truck as an extra utility vehicle when he was building his new home and had found that it came in so handy that although he had another regular use vehicle, he kept it around for those times when you just need a truck . . . or have a hankering to look manly.

I timidly approached Luis after church and asked politely if there was any possibility that I could borrow his truck to move my household furnishings. He beamed such a warm smile and responded so positively that it actually made me feel a bit wary. *I wonder what kind of favor in return I am setting myself up for here?* my suspicious mind thought. *Will I have to watch his kids for a weekend? Listen to a time-share pitch? Take his dogs for a walk? Pledge my son to marry his daughter?*

I shook off those darker thoughts and arranged to pick up his truck on the following weekend.

Luis's truck was an older-model full-size Ford with a nice lumber rack on it. The car had seen some duty but was in pristine shape.

"Use it as long as you need to," said Luis as he tossed me the keys.

I used Luis's truck to move all the stuff I had collected over the years. I made a number of trips, dragging our belongings from house to house.

A little later I used Luis's truck to haul middle school kid's gear to camp. Then I used Luis's truck to take junk to the dump.

Each time, Luis would offer up his truck with warm generosity.

Often I would see Luis's fully loaded truck maneuvering down the road. The driver was seldom Luis. Instead, it was some friend or friend of a friend who heard that Luis had a truck he would loan out. And while most of us returned the vehicle with a full tank of gas and a thank-you, Luis paid for tires, maintenance and insurance out of his own pocket.

And contrary to my cloudy suspicions, Luis never asked for a favor in return. The loan of his truck was without condition, expectation or presumption.

His simple gesture of a truck loan inspired me.

Yes, it was part of his collection of stuff, but Luis had figured out how to have a light grip on it. Luis's truck was not there for the pure enjoyment, industry and satisfaction of Luis or his close friends and family; it was there for the higher good. It was there for those who needed a truck but had neither the money to rent one nor the connections to borrow one.

It was a truck owned by Luis but held in common for the sake of the Kingdom. In fact, I don't think Luis saw himself as the owner at all; he was merely the steward for a truck truly owned by Jesus.

Utopian ponderings, long nailed shut, began to resurrect in my mind. *What if I approached my stuff with truly the same attitude that Luis had with his truck? Owned by me, but held in common for the sake of the Kingdom.*

I felt my hand of ownership loosen, my approach to "things" alter.

We ended up moving houses three times in three years—a long, convoluted process that would finally end in our being able to move into a newly constructed home of our own design.

During the last of those moves, I convinced my wife that I needed to buy my own used truck, and I have tried hard to model my ownership of that truck on the way Luis handled his truck.

It is often absent from my yard. Even as I peck out these words, my truck is in a neighbor's driveway being loaded up with green waste.

And my truck, along with my new home, my money, my toys, gear, food and anything else that can be labeled as "stuff," is not mine; it is owned by Jesus. And until He returns, He lets me use it not only for myself but expects me to also use it for the common good.

So, to update an old psalm, I hope it can be said in truth that the Lord owns the trucks in a thousand driveways.

But that being the case, I think I know which one He would drive. It would be mine: a manly, four-wheel drive, full-bed V-8, lifted, with big oversized tires.

Jesus would look good in it.

Here's the lesson: Use your worldly resources to benefit others and make friends. Then, when your earthly possessions are gone, they will welcome you to an eternal home.

Luke 16:9, *NLT*

I've never, as you so well know, had any taste for wealth or fashion. With these bare hands I took care of my own basic needs and those who worked with me. In everything I've done, I have demonstrated to you how necessary it is to work on behalf of the weak and not exploit them. You'll not likely go wrong here if you keep remembering that our Master said, "You're far happier giving than getting."

Acts 20:33-35, *THE MESSAGE*

8

A LESSON FROM THAT ANNOYING SIGN GUY

For most of my Christian journey I have tried very hard not to be a spiritual snob. I strain to be generous to believers whose practices and theology I privately think are a bit loopy. I understand intellectually that none of us has even remotely got it all figured out right, and that our sovereign God has and may continue to use complete idiots, of which I may be chief.

I know that in one part of my mind.

But to be honest, another part of me really wants to look down my nose at the antics of some fellow believers or, even better, ridicule them out loud and creatively . . . in public.

This is not for the run-of-the-mill Christian craziness; one could keep busy all day long lampooning the mismatched actions and ideologies that are paraded around as normal Christianity. I save my thunder for the really nutty stuff. And even though I know it may not be terribly loving, understanding or kind, every once in a while I give in to temptation and go on a rant (usually of a humorous kind) about some kooky behavior or idea being served up as Christian by some clown near the lunatic fringe of our community.

And I think you would agree with me that some of these people really deserve to be lampooned.

The pompous, big-haired, diamond-ringed, Rolex-wearing televangelist touring a third-world country, and uncomfortably bouncing a clueless little orphan kid on his Gucci pants for just as long as the video camera rolls, is a joke to anyone but himself and a few thousand mindless but donating devotees.

Christian recording artists who, after they get sufficient notoriety to cross over to the secular realm, have the nerve to show disdain to the very audience who made their success possible deserve to have their inflated egos meet the pushpin of satire.

The shysters who spend their God-given imagination coming up with wild and even weird ways to fleece the sheep by promising miracle cures and overflowing wallets to those dumb enough to send in their checks. (P. T. Barnum is attributed to have said, "No one has ever gone broke underestimating the intelligence of the American public." I think it may go double for the Christian public.)

This is classic pharisaical behavior, and I think poking fun at it is not only apt but the model Jesus Himself used to good effect on spiritual buffoons. Reading some of those broadsides the Master delivered is almost like reading a comedy routine, and I would wager that the crowds that heard Jesus deliver them snickered at His delicious wordplays and send-ups.

Some Christians are not so much hypocritical as they are annoying, odd and, on many occasions, embarrassing to most of us "normal" people.

I remember as a born and bred Southern California beach kid, every once in a while during our lazy summers by the ocean there would arrive Christian kids from the Midwest whose leaders had decided it would be a good idea to go west and evangelize tanned, salty pagans such as myself.

From a distance you could see them hiking along the sand line, usually traveling in pairs, their white skin contrasting with their dark socks and shoes.

Our gang would watch the odd parade picking their way across the sand with mild curiosity.

"Who are these strange aliens that don't have the sense to lose their shoes at the beach?" we would ponder. "Why are the girls wearing so much clothing, and what are they doing approaching us?"

"Witnessing" is, of course, what they thought they were doing. "Entertaining" is what they were actually doing—as any of our crew who didn't drift off after realizing we had been marked simply played with these clueless invaders who transgressed our turf without invitation—until we tired of their canned high-pressure Christian sales pitch.

Years later, as a Christian, and a youth worker in those same Southern California beach areas, I found that summer would still bring a small trickle of similar evangelists to the places where I worked, surfed and cruised with students.

I would lower and slowly shake my head in embarrassment—for them and for our common faith—because *I knew better* how to deliver the message. You see, I had made it my life's work to reach out to unsaved teens who were just like I was growing up, and I was darn sure that the message was being killed by the cultural clumsiness of the messenger.

This violation isn't limited to the cool crew at the beach. I felt the same way about the strange people I saw dragging a cross through downtown Denver at lunchtime and who, after setting up on a street corner, spiritually harangued hungry business people as they went out to graze. Nobody said anything—most avoided eye contact—but you could almost see the thought bubbles reading, "Get a life, Bub!" (among the kinder sentiments) as they passed by.

But I especially felt that way about the clown who held up the hand-lettered John 3:16 sign at every televised sporting event.

I suspected that there was not one clown doing this but a whole Christian circus full of these guys who pay big bucks for prime seats not to watch a game but to get their message out on national television without having to pay a dime.

The sign guy annoyed me.

He made it hard for me to concentrate on the game as he popped up here and there flailing his placard.

"What a mutt!" I would grumble under my breath to no one in particular every time the camera accidentally caught him.

Sometimes a friend with a gentle spirit would be watching a game with me. When I would go on a rant, my friend would slip in a word in a vain attempt to defuse my cynicism.

"I wouldn't do it that way, but you know, it's all worth it if someone gets saved," the friend would say.

"Yeah? Do you know anyone who has gotten saved by the John 3:16 guy?" I would retort. "Well, what about the ton of guys who write off Jesus because of the antics of this guy?"

Self-righteousness is so much fun. Especially when you are so obviously right.

One day, Dain, a young surf guy, showed up at our church on Sunday morning. Smart, handsome, articulate and well educated, he had renounced his goal of living in the business world fast lane when, as a college senior, his grandfather dropped dead in front of him. He had spent his post-college years as a brilliant and likeable adventurer, traveling the world for good surf while picking up a mild drug habit and a different girl in every port.

He had the kind of life many people dream about.

The problem was, it wasn't quite working for him. Something or *someone* was missing.

As time went on, and his faith grew, he became part of the worship band, then a leader of the worship band; then after a stint in Bible School, part of our church staff.

I had heard tidbits, over the years, of his encounter with Christ. I knew that he had little church influence growing up. I knew that he had bumped into various Christian surfers here and there, but none of them claimed to be the driving influence in the conversion of Dain.

It seemed like one of those curious *God only* situations that drew him toward Jesus. Stranger stuff has happened.

One day, I asked him what the turning point was. How it was that he knew where to look to fill the spiritual void.

"Well, I was feeling really empty inside," Dain said. "I knew I needed God, but I didn't quite know where to start. So I decided to sit down and watch a football game . . . and have you ever seen that John 3:16 sign that some guy always holds up . . . ?"

The thudding sound that followed was my jaw dropping to the table.

It couldn't be! I thought. *No! No! Dain was far too suave, smart and world experienced to have taken that bait!*

But it was true.

Dain got up from the game, somehow found a Bible and turned for the first time to those simple, beautiful words that every Christian knows by heart.

Kneeling, he surrendered his life to Jesus and began the journey of transformation.

"I always thought that sign guy was such an annoying jerk!" I said.

Dain gave a bright smile and then, with palms up and opened wide, he shrugged his shoulders.

I walked away from our conversation spitting crow feathers. I had been massively humbled. And I was stunned at the unpredictability of the Almighty.

I didn't go out and make a John 3:16 sign, nor did I change my view that there are some forms of sharing the gospel that are *generally*, at least in my mind, much more palatable than others.

But that very day I did shut up about the sign guy and most of his ilk. The revelation also made me come to the conclusion that my lofty opinions may not be worth all that much in the end—especially when God is lurking about.

But God chose the foolish things of the world to shame the wise;
God chose the weak things of the world to shame the strong.
He chose the lowly things of this world and the despised things—
and the things that are not—to nullify the things that are.

1 Corinthians 1:27-28, *NIV*

"Master," said John, "we saw a man driving out demons
in your name and we tried to stop him, because he is not one of us."
"Do not stop him," Jesus said,
"for whoever is not against you is for you."

Luke 9:49-50, *NIV*

God told Moses, "I'm in charge of mercy. I'm in charge of compas-
sion." Compassion doesn't originate in our bleeding hearts or
moral sweat, but in God's mercy. The same point was made when
God said to Pharaoh, "I picked you as a bit player in this drama of
my salvation power." All we're saying is that God has the first
word, initiating the action in which we play our part for good or ill.

Romans 9:15-18, *THE MESSAGE*

9

THE DAY I HAD MOST OF KEN'S LIFE IN MY CAR

I happened to be hanging out in Southern California when tinder-dry sagebrush ignited under hot Santa Ana winds.

For those who reside in that state, this is not a particularly unique event. They tend to take it in stride, like Northerners take horrible blizzards or Southerners hurricanes.

Most of the time these fires are in remote areas, and if they do creep into someplace more developed they tend to be beaten back by daring fire personnel after gobbling up a home or two.

Those losses, while tragic, are most often small and isolated.

While in San Diego, to be part of the Youth Specialties National Youth Workers Convention, I accepted the invitation of my friend Ken to camp out at the comfortable home he and his wife, Jeanie, shared in the not too distant hills of Escondido. Home-brewed coffee, free big screen TV with a subwoofer that bounced you off the sofa, a snuggly bed and good comradeship beat a hotel room any day.

After the meetings, I went out with friends and fed my Mexican-food addiction and then wheeled back to Ken's home for the night.

Even though it was late, Ken and his wife were up watching local news on the television. A slight bit of worry etched their faces.

"Wassup?" I inquired as I came through the door.

"They have a kind of nasty fire going off way to the east of us," Ken said. "My son and his family live out there, so if they don't get it under control, they just might have to evacuate."

"Bummer," I said, contemplating for a few seconds what it might be like to have to pack everything that means anything to you into your car and let the rest burn.

"They'll probably get it under control," I said. "They usually do."

Ken and Jeanie nodded. They were pros. Every few years fire rampages somewhere around the area, many of the fires set intentionally by cretins who run out with a book of matches as soon the famous Santa Ana winds start to blow dry air up from the desert toward the sea.

The Mexican feast settling in my stomach was making me sleepy, so I bid my friends good evening, jumped into the shower and then hit the sack, dropping to sleep quickly and peacefully.

Just after 3:00 A.M., I was awakened to the sound of voices, both adult and children's, that I did not recognize. It was dark, and for a moment I was disoriented in a strange house and bed. Then I realized that this must be Ken and Jeanie's family seeking safety from the fire that was approaching their home.

Wow, must be scary for them, I thought to myself groggily.

I settled back under the covers and drifted back to sleep.

Morning did not dawn. The alarm went off, but what light there was slipping through the blinds seemed dulled and shaded.

This is strange, I thought to myself. Then I picked up the smell of campfire.

Springing out of bed, I slid disheveled into the living room. Ken and his entire family were there, the adults glued to the television and the small kids running amuck as if they were on a great adventure.

"Rick, looks like you aren't going anywhere . . . they just closed the Interstate!" was the morning welcome I was greeted with.

I stood there dumfounded.

Out the window I could see the sky was thick with gray-brown smoke. The wind howled and the air was full of leaves and ashes.

I was scheduled to be a presenter at the conference; so I quickly dialed the promoters and let them know that I was stuck due to the inferno that had rapidly spread overnight.

I returned to the family and joined in a bit of their angst.

"What are you going to do?" I asked.

"We'll stay put until we are told we have to leave," said Ken.

Frankly, I was ready to make an exit at that moment. I had little investment involved; a small suitcase and a rental car were the only responsibilities that I had. But for my friend, well, he had a house full of memories and goods. He wasn't going to be stampeded out of his castle easily.

The wind picked up intensity outside and I heard a sharp crack as a huge limb snapped off a tree and collapsed in the front yard.

The velocity of the fire-driven wind was slowly denuding other trees, and I could see that this wildfire had coupled with the natural winds to produce a classic firestorm.

Ironically, the fact that I had virtually zero investment in Ken's home or Ken's stuff (other than friendship) slowly put me in an almost detached state of mind. I was clearheaded, unemotional and extremely objective.

I knew my friend well enough to see that he was putting on a good face for his wife and kids, but underneath his skin panic was starting to erupt.

Then the call came.

For those with landlines, it is called a reverse 911. Ken had gone all cell, so it was a neighbor who came over and broke the news. The authorities had ordered the whole area to be evacuated within 20 minutes.

Ken and Jeanie's kids got out quickly. They had already been through this drill once and their minivan was still packed with all the worldly goods they could stuff into it from that evening's evacuation. They grabbed their children and headed for the evacuation route, leaving Ken, Jeanie and me behind to load everything of importance into two small vehicles.

I stood in the entryway of their house, watching my friends actually do in real life what many of us have done only in a speculative discussion.

"What would you grab if there was a fire?" is one of those theoretical questions that are asked at parties because while we know it *could* happen, most of us realize that it never will.

Now, for Ken and Jeanie, the nightmare was real. Twenty minutes to decide and get out . . . maybe less.

The couple scurried around each room, many times coming out with nothing and then going back in again to reassess.

I opened up the back end of my rental car and tried to pack in the things they brought out to me as economically as possible.

What they brought out was, in some ways, what you would expect; the photo albums and pictures from off the wall. Ken brought me his computer (leaving the fancy display screen and keyboard). It had years of work, contacts and information hiding in the 1s and 0s.

A crate appeared with file folders and important papers. I wedged it into the backseat.

When I went back into the house, I saw Jeanie brush her hand along the side of her black grand piano. She is a worship leader at her church and has the rare gift of perfect pitch. The piano is her main tool, but it would stay.

Ken emerged from his office with a guitar, one of many that he owns and in dollar value worth far less than any of them.

"I made this myself," he said, handing it to me.

It would be one of only two guitars that found refuge in my car.

In Ken and Jeanie's car went practical things in the event they became homeless gypsies; clothes, dog food for their big black lab, blankets and a couple of pillows. Their little car filled quickly.

The sky now had lost most of its dark gray and I could see orange and yellow light from the flames flicker just behind the hills. This thing was coming our way and the escape clock was running down.

I asked Ken if he had a camera. And while they chased around, I snapped photos of the home, the yard, and the ominously and oddly beautiful sky. I wanted to document what they had together, not so much for their insurance company (although for that purpose it is very helpful) but for their memories.

In the final minutes, I took the fly-on-the-wall role of watching the couple revisit all the rooms of their house and exit clutching a small box of overlooked pictures from the wall.

"We gotta go!" said Ken. As I turned to follow him out of his house, I noticed his wife doing something interesting; she washed and dried a coffee mug that had been left from breakfast, putting it away in the cupboard, and then wiped down the sink and faucet.

"Why did you do that?" I asked, thinking that if the house burned down, having all your cups and plates clean and in the right spot wouldn't matter.

"I don't know," she said, somewhat in amazement of her own behavior.

(I personally think this was her small statement of hope and defiance of the danger that loomed nearby. "I will be back," her actions seemed to say.)

We stood outside the house and prayed that God might spare this home, trusting that His mercy might outweigh the mechanics of His natural creation. Then we jumped into our cars and fired them up. Ken and Jeanie were going to try to find shelter with some friends in Los Angeles, and I decided to try to find a way along the Pacific Coast Highway into San Diego. We agreed to keep in contact, if possible, so that Ken would know the whereabouts of his gear.

Driving alone through the smoke so thick that it looked like fog, and seeping into the car so that my clothing smelled as if I had been suspended over a barbeque, a thought came to me: *I have most of Ken's life in the back of my car.*

His memories and mementoes bounced together in the backseat. His ideas, information and years of effort were crowded into the trunk. The tools that he used to bring joy, to lead worship and to translate creativity snuggled tightly together across the seat.

These were the "things" that he valued. And of course, those "things" took a distant second place to people—his wife, his children and grandchildren.

It sure got me thinking.

When you can reduce the entire contents of your life into what would fit into a couple small sedans, well it makes you ponder what is of real value.

As I thought about it, the things I hauled around with me as I sought my way out of smoke and ash represented the things that truly mean something to us all: the memories of loved ones in faded pictures, and small keepsakes. Celebrations of love shared in old wedding photos and of couples entwined on warm distant sands. And our identities: little bits of paper that prove who we are, where we came from and what we have done. The strings of connections to friends, made up of phone numbers and email addresses, and the fruit of our creativity held in a computer disk.

Later that evening, I rendezvoused with Ken in a mall parking lot and we transferred his life from my car to his.

Several days later he was able to return to his home, the fire narrowly missing his housing tract.

And I flew home.

As the plane banked up and over the ocean, I peeked out the window and saw the smoke from the now subsiding fire blanket the ocean for miles.

Sitting in my own living room later that day, I made mental notes on what I would grab in case of a fire and found my list interestingly close to the things that I had helped load out of Ken's home.

I found that I wanted to hang out with my family, to stay in bed a little longer and snuggle with my wife, to call a few friends I hadn't called for a while, and to jot down a thank-you note or two.

For weeks afterwards I replayed the tape of that last 20 minutes at Ken's house in my mind. I realized that while I had total objectivity at the time, the events affected me later on.

Most everything I have spent time and money on will end up rusting in the dump, victim to the ravages of time. The achievements, the great ideas, sooner or later will lay unnoticed, uncared for and unappreciated.

But some things do last—things of a spiritual nature. Things that come from the heart of God that end up going right back to Him with a little of me attached to each: love, creativity, care, friendship.

Carrying Ken's life around in the back of my car made me want to grab at those kinds of things that no fire, no passage of time, no flood, no worm or human indifference can destroy.

As for man, his days are like grass, he flourishes like
a flower of the field; the wind blows over it and it is gone,
and its place remembers it no more.

Psalm 103:15-16, *NIV*

A man's life does not consist in the abundance of his possessions.

Luke 12:15, *NIV*

Don't hoard treasure down here where it gets eaten by moths
and corroded by rust or—worse!—stolen by burglars.
Stockpile treasure in heaven, where it's safe from moth and rust
and burglars. It's obvious, isn't it? The place where your treasure
is, is the place you will most want to be, and end up being.

Matthew 6:19-21, *THE MESSAGE*

10

NIMBYS AND THE
LOVE OF JESUS

There was a folded notice in my mailbox. Everyone in our little neighborhood got one. It was a ranting alarm piece telling of a real and present danger to the safety of my family and the security of my property value.

"They" were coming to the neighborhood.

Little did I know on that sunny afternoon when I pulled the notice from my mailbox that I was on a collision course with most of the folks on my block and with some of my dear and wonderful Christian friends.

Like a car accident, these social impacts come right out of nowhere and leave everyone shaken.

But the probability of a collision should be expected, especially for Christians.

One of the things that make Jesus so interesting is that He really messes with our orderly little world.

He won't leave good enough alone.

He demolishes our flimsy constructs and bulldozes our excuses and justifications.

I like how He screwed around with people's thinking.

To the guys trying to put Him in a lose/lose situation with a tricky tax question, He simply asked them to flip Him a coin and then said, "Give to Caesar what belongs to Caesar and to God what belongs to God" (see Luke 20:25), leaving them to figure out which was which.

There is a hierarchy of value in the economy of the Kingdom. People matter more than stuff, family matters more than people, God matters more than family, and everyone matters more than self.

So what does belong to Caesar anyway?

God gets close and personal, butting in about matters such as finances, family and how we treat our neighbors or potential neighbors.

The note in the mailbox was a call to arms. According to the information contained in it, the state, which by chance owned one small house in the neighborhood, was going to make it a halfway house that would no doubt house brutal criminals. Prison over-crowding was to blame.

No one would be safe! Children and small animals would have to be kept indoors; everyone would have to buy firearms, large fe-rocious dogs, alarm systems and create a safe room.

Not only that, but we were going to see our property value crash through the floor as the neighborhood became the destina-tion of choice for the flotsam of society.

A public meeting at the neighborhood center was called.

I had obligations that evening but thought I could pop in for 45 minutes and see what all the ruckus was about.

In the meantime, I did a little research on my own.

I found that the state did indeed own a house up the street from me and that an agency was contemplating the possibility of putting a few kids (not adult criminals) who were chronic run-aways into a home situation with 24/7 adult supervision.

It was hard to find parking at the neighborhood center. A nerve had been touched.

The flyer had done its job; the neighbors had, for the most part, already made up their minds. In fact, the scene resembled a townsfolk mob scene out of an old movie. Only the torches and pitchforks were missing.

There were many Christians in the room. A good number of them came from my own church. They were mostly quiet and polite.

So was I . . . at least for a while.

The representatives for the state were outnumbered and out-gunned. They tried to outline the fact that they were merely look-ing for a neighborhood location to place a home for boys with minor problems. They quickly went over the particulars, which made it obvious that this kind of living situation is highly regulated and supervised.

In fact, the presenters made it quite clear that after surveying the house under consideration, they considered it to be too close to the next-door home to fit the proposed use.

None of this mattered to the crowd.

The reaction was quick and hostile.

I was shocked by the ferocity of the people I knew or was at least acquainted with. And I was even more surprised by the murmuring approval of my brothers and sisters in the room.

I had done some thinking about the whole situation.

I care about my neighbors and I understand the fear of opening the door to reprobates and unsavory elements. I have seen perfectly wonderful family neighborhoods dissolve into dangerous no-go zones.

Like my neighbors, I have more than a bit of equity and future security tied up in the value of my home.

And, like my neighbors, I cared deeply about the safety of my wife and kids and would do whatever was necessary to protect them.

But unlike most of my secular neighbors, I have one other element to interject into a decision like this: the will of my Master, Jesus.

The more I thought about it the more I became certain that my role as a believer in the neighborhood was to keep an open heart and open door to kids such as these. The fingerprints of Jesus are all over the issue of how we treat those who the world considers a problem.

It seemed to me that we were asking the wrong questions.

Instead of asking how we could keep these miscreants out of our neighborhood, we should be asking if it would be possible to invite the kids over for a barbeque. Instead of being fearful that our kids would be getting harassed or tempted at the school bus stop, we should be asking for the names of these kids so we can pray for them and muse on how to expose them to our faith . . . in advance. Instead of asking if our property value will take a dive, we should be asking if we have enough room in our backyard to put up a half-court basketball court for the kids to use.

I went to the meeting figuring that my brothers and sisters had done some hard thinking too and might be asking the right questions as well.

I did not intend to speak. I wanted only fly-on-the-wall status and, besides, I had to buzz off quickly for another commitment.

I was disappointed that the Christians within earshot verbally applauded each speaker who whined of disaster and doom for our neighborhood.

I was stunned when those who I knew to be hardcore liberals rose to do a fine series of Cheshire Cat imitations and smilingly (and disingenuously) claimed that they really do think it is important for wayward children to be welcomed in a neighborhood but that this particular one was not quite "the right fit." I was disappointed as I thought for sure that those who held far left views would be offering more than lip service cheerleading for a teen halfway house . . . anywhere but here.

In fact, it all boiled down to the cry, "Not in my backyard!" (NIMBY).

Yes! There is a need; yes, someone has to help these kids; yes, they should be in a neighborhood surrounded by normal families who would model a lifestyle they could aspire to . . . but not in the vicinity of our homes!

I held my tongue under a discouraging barrage of nonsense attempting to disguise itself as genuine caring.

Finally, one neighbor pulled off his soft gloves. Standing to speak he declared, "These kind of people are a cancer put in our neighborhood that will infect and destroy others who come in contact with it."

Something inside of me snapped. Perhaps it was the image of a small crew of messed-up kids being equated to malicious cancer that rocketed me to my feet.

"I live in this neighborhood," I said. "I have a wife and two school-age kids at home, and I am just as concerned as anyone here about their safety and welfare. But I have to tell you, right now I am very ashamed of many of my friends and neighbors."

I went on to say that I thought our neighborhood would be a perfect place for kids who were struggling and that we should be thinking about how we could impact these kids' lives instead of how we could banish them from our neighborhoods. I reminded them that everyone says they want to help unfortunate kids like these, as long as they don't come near our backyard.

I guess you could say I preached at them, the churchgoers and the non-churchgoers alike. I used both barrels.

I hoped it would end up like one of those often-used movie scenes where after one brave soul gives a rousing speech the mood of the crowd suddenly changes and the hostile mob, having seen the light, is transformed into a bunch of cheering supporters.

Instead, nobody said anything; but a bunch of them scowled at me. My friends turned away their heads; some cleared their throats as if they had just witnessed a performance by the village idiot.

I looked at my watch and realized I had to go.

A funny thing happened to me as I drove away that night, something that has never happened to me before: I was crushed with grief for my Christian friends and neighbors.

I had a terrible feeling that as a Christian leader and Bible teacher, I had somehow let them down. I felt that their lack of moral clarity on this subject was somehow my fault. I had been trying to teach and lead them for years, and they still couldn't see a way to come up with the godly answer to such an obvious problem.

In standing up for the idea of placing a halfway home in our neighborhood, I had managed to anger and alienate most of the families on the block.

One person did call me with an encouraging word, telling me that I was right on in what I said. Ironically, he was an unbeliever.

Most of the saints said nothing to me, but it was obvious that they grumbled about my little sermon privately.

I was and still am convinced that in spite of my plunging popularity in the neighborhood, this was a hill worth dying on. It is an odd sensation to find oneself standing all alone on what appears to be the high moral ground.

In the end, the issue of the halfway house turned out to be only an academic question. The state had already decided that the home itself was not appropriate.

But in some ways it was more than an academic question floated over wine and cheese where the enlightened minds strive to present themselves as sophisticated and genteel.

It was more than a case study that was kicked around in a Bible study—more than a question that could be answered with spiritual confidence from the comfort of a soft couch—for the very reason that it was merely a question that nothing actually hinged upon.

These are places where it is safe to give the "right" answer.

The dilemma of the halfway house was real and gritty. It was a place where the rhetoric of Christianity touched the powerful impulse to be safe, secure and protective.

In truth, it was pretty easy for me to be the voice crying in the wilderness of this issue. After all, I spent decades as a youth worker. I am not fearful of even the toughest of them and have a knee-jerk instinct to reach out to kids who are hurting.

But I do wonder if I would have the courage to make the same speech about a convicted sex offender who wanted to move into the neighborhood. Does Jesus want me to love him any less because he has a horrific perversion? I wonder if I would hold my tongue if a huge family of strange foreigners with weird customs, strange and smelly food and bizarre religious practices wanted to move in . . . and encourage their family and friends to immigrate to the neighborhood as well. Would I welcome Jehovah's Witnesses with their ties, briefcases, darkened house on every holiday and obvious disdain for professional clergy such as I?

Sometimes it is easy to plant our flag on the moral high ground. Sometimes we can't even lay our hands on the flag, let alone figure out where the moral high ground is.

Pastor Martin Niemöller was an early supporter of Adolph Hitler. After all, the country was in economic shambles and many of Hitler's ideas appealed to the common man (he did produce the "People's Car," better known as the Volkswagen, remember?). The pastor was not even terribly bothered by the anti-Semitic pronouncements of the party, as this kind of talk was as normal to him growing up as segregated drinking fountains were to people growing up in the Southern states during the early 1900s.

In time, the ideas of the Nazi regime would begin to rub harder against Pastor Martin's maturing Christian faith. Slowly, he began to voice quiet criticism and distance himself from the government. Before war erupted, Niemöller had become thoroughly disillusioned with Hitler and the Nazi party. He joined with other vocal Christian opponents, most of whom were arrested and executed before the fall of Germany. Niemöller himself ended up in a concentration camp, narrowly avoiding death. Shortly after the war he wrote an oft-quoted verse, "First They Came . . ." about his own initial complacency during that turbulent time:

> First they came for the Communists, and I didn't speak up because I wasn't a Communist.
> Then they came for the mentally ill, the so-called incurables and I didn't speak up, because I wasn't mentally ill.
> Then they came for the Jews, and I didn't speak up because I wasn't a Jew.
> Then they came for me, and by that time there was no one left to speak up.

I am afraid that it may be an important exercise for all of us to do some mental dress rehearsal to figure out what is the Christian thing to do, think or say before we are faced with the dilemma.

What will I speak up for? What will I defend? For what will I be willing to alienate friends, family and neighbors? What will be my response if I am cheated out of money, have a friend who starts an adulterous relationship, lose my job to an unscrupulous competitor, or be accused of something I am innocent of? Can my convictions be bought, bullied or swayed, and am I absolutely sure that my convictions are the same ones Jesus would share?

Here is a simple rule of thumb for behavior: Ask yourself what you want people to do for you; then grab the initiative and do it for them! If you only love the lovable, do you expect a pat on the back? Run-of-the-mill sinners do that. If you only help those who help you, do you expect a medal? Garden-variety sinners do that. If you only give for what you hope to get out of it, do you think that's charity? The stingiest of pawnbrokers does that.

Luke 6:31-34, *THE MESSAGE*

So cut away the thick calluses from your heart and stop being so willfully hardheaded. GOD, your God, is the God of all gods, he's the Master of all masters, a God immense and powerful and awesome. He doesn't play favorites, takes no bribes, makes sure orphans and widows are treated fairly, takes loving care of foreigners by seeing that they get food and clothing.

Deuteronomy 10:16-19, *THE MESSAGE*

11

THE HOLY BOOK ON TOP

My friend who works at a major bookstore chain told me that when he loads books on the shelves in the religion section he is not allowed to put any book above the Koran—the holy book of Islam.

I didn't really believe him, so I made it a point to check out the location of the Koran every time I go to one of those bookstores.

Sure enough, there it sits on the top shelf.

The reason was that either through pressure or threat of pressure (or worse) from Islamic groups, the bookstore has agreed to the demand that the Koran be treated "above" all other religious books by placing it on the top shelf.

Meanwhile, the various translations of the Bible occupy shelves on a lower level.

It is amazing what a public relations department can accomplish when it can conjure up people who will strap a bomb on themselves for their cause.

If this "policy" got any media play, it would really annoy a lot of people, especially people who claim to have a profound reverence for the Bible and would prefer that *it* get top billing in the bookstore.

It annoys me, too, but primarily because I hate to see capitulation of this kind to fears real or imagined; and when I'm in these bookstores I always do my bit against terroristic threatening by moving the Koran down a shelf or two when nobody is looking.

But I haven't gone so far as to load the top shelf with Bibles. Yet.

When I was growing up, we had a Bible in our house. It was old and thick, with pimply black leather. The embossed golden lettering on the spine boldly declared: *Holy Bible*.

It sat on the back edge of a coffee table, and you were not allowed to set anything on top it.

The Bible was holy in a *magical* type of way for us kids; people put their hands on it in court, kids swore on an imaginary stack of them, adults wrote their family lineage in them and sometimes pressed flowers in their heavy pages. The family Bible was a holy keepsake, a consecrated paperweight.

We dusted it and treated it with reverence, but nobody I knew ever picked it up and actually read it.

In a religious way it had similarities to the copy of the United States Constitution that my mom, in a patriotic mood, pinned to our bedroom wall; it was something every red-blooded American said they would fight for but few knew more than a few lines from.

If we had taken the time to read the old family Bible, we would have found language more in common with the works of Shakespeare than what was spoken at the corner market or schoolyard. And we would have quickly abandoned the attempt to navigate its language and consigned it to the list of ancient books that only dusty academics have any inclination to read.

There was nothing within the pages of the Bible to help guide the novice to understand which books were accounts of history, which were songs, which were civil law and which were dramas.

Titles were confusing or antiquated; personal letters were termed "epistles" and biographies were called "Gospels."

In short, the Bible was strange, foreboding and inaccessible.

Oh, and did I say irrelevant?

I grew up with an attitude toward the Bible similar to that I have toward lima beans: *tried 'em once, didn't like 'em; if you do, you can have mine.*

The Bible has fallen on hard times.

Preachers used to make ultimate authority for their case by thrusting a finger in the Book while declaring, "The Bible says . . ."

That phrase once got people quivering, but nowadays the reaction is merely a "So what?" shrug. The authority of the Bible has evaporated in the minds of the populace as they sink into the goo of relativism.

In fact, taking a good whack at the authority and reliability of the Bible (and, in turn, those Neanderthals who still believe in it) has become somewhat of a sport.

"Experts" and "scholars" create color-coded Bibles so that you can know which of the words of Jesus really came from His lips and which were inserted later by some wild-eyed scribe or special-interest group. A short read of these "authentic" words of Christ turn out to be a toothless and smarmy collection of "love everybody" platitudes, making Him sound more like an ancient hippie than anything else.

Popular books demeaning God, the Bible, et al, have become bestsellers and get their authors spots on the kind of talk shows where they can debate the least capable defenders of the Christian faith the network can locate.

Cherry-picking some passage (almost always out of context) and using it as a sample of the kind of thing that makes the Bible out of date or even worse—intolerant and malevolent—is standard fare among the enlightened and clucked in repetition by other parrots.

The attempt to lay the violence of history at the feet of the Bible and the loons who propagate it is common rhetoric in cyber space, on college campuses and in the airwaves.

And if you want to have real fun at a party, just mention how much you admire those missionaries who go into untouched cultures and translate the Bible into the vernacular.

It is like spitting on the hors d'oeuvre tray.

Christians all too often have not helped much.

Some die-hard *King James* fans scratch and claw to come up with reasons why this particular English translation is, and always will be, God's favorite.

Some act ungraciously to those who may not agree with them on some less than essential viewpoint about the Bible, almost coming to blows over the question of whether the book of Job is parabolic theater or the recounting of actual events, or if Genesis creation "days" are describing 24-hour time periods or epochs.

Marketing departments of Bible publishers have recast this universal text into niche corners with such interesting offerings as: The Surfers Bibles (sand included), The Cowboy Bible (read with your spurs on), The Adventure Bible (finally, a chance to wear your pith helmet), The Inmate Bible (goes nicely with stripes) and, of course, a New Testament for lesbians, gays, bisexuals and trans-gendereds (no, I am not kidding).

Kinda makes you feel like the Bible can be stretched to fit just about any lifestyle or ideology as long as there is money to be made.

Modern technology has caused fits in some quarters.

Is a Bible app on an iPhone the appropriate thing to use or is there something sacred about ink and paper? Does projecting a passage on the wall during a worship service cause biblical illiteracy because people will no longer bring their Bibles with them on Sunday morning?

And then there are those who are tempted to worship the Bible with equal fervor as the One of whom it speaks.

As I recall, Jesus warned against the "house divided" approach (see Mark 3:25).

In spite of all this static, I, for one, really love to read the Bible, but I have to admit, not having read the Good Book before, it baffled me right out of the gate.

I had been a Christian only a short time and decided to plunge into the New Testament like one would do any normal book—start at the front and work your way to the end.

Matthew's opening lines would not have won any award as a literary pacesetter, and they came very close to driving me away at first glance. But I decided to apply my well-tested reading method to these initial pages: *When it is boring, skip over it.* Pretty soon I was sucked into the story and the words of Jesus.

I read well into the night; and within a day or so, I had devoured what I would later understand to be the Gospels. But as I read I found myself in a state of mental confusion. I kept feeling like I had read the same thing before, but kinda different.

No one had bothered to explain to me that the first four books of the New Testament were telling the same story from different perspectives. (By the way, these are the kinds of things that are really helpful to point out to novice Bible readers.)

Over the years I read the Bible a lot.

I tried to memorize chunks of it but was a miserable failure. I found I could remember the gist of the passage but, without fail, could not get it down word perfect or have any shred of hope in recalling the address.

Not a great portent for someone who would later become a pastor.

Note of confession: I still cannot memorize worth a darn or recall the address of a well-used verse. (It also took me several decades to memorize my social security number, so I think there is a pattern here.)

I got over thinking that the Bible itself was some kind of mystical holy book to be treated with top-of-the-shelf reverence. I marked mine up, scribbled in the margins, threw it in the trash when all the pages started falling out and started with a fresh new one. I put my coffee mug on top of it and freely tossed it on the backseat of my truck.

I began to see the Bible as God's tool to tell a holy story and not as a coffee table talisman.

I even went to Bible school. (Clueless as ever, I was later astonished to find that the nice elderly British professor who allowed me to sit on the floor of his bedroom and pepper him with questions actually had lots of books published under his name: F. F. Bruce.)

The Bible tells God's story of pursuit and love for fallen humans. It is paper and ink; it is the electronic dance of letters on a computer screen. It is light bending through stained glass windows or thick lines of a child's coloring book. It is a verbal retelling around a smoky campfire or at a youth meeting. It tells a holy story and teaches holy precepts, but it is not all that particular about the vehicle used.

On the numerous occasions I have to sit at the sickbed of a person whose days are numbered, it is with distinct clarity that they ask me to read the words of hope from the Bible.

I have never had a request for Nietzsche.

No family member who has lost a loved one has clamored to hear from Darwin about the survival of the fittest, but they do cling to words penned thousands of years ago that breathe the breath of God.

None of the broken lives I have seen mended have done so because of a good dose of Sartre or the acid wit of Bertrand Russell. But I know many for whom the message of grace from the Bible was a healing salve.

Time and time again, in culture after culture, the wisdom displayed in the Bible has proven itself to be a divinely designed operating manual for living a life full of mercy, grace, love, kindness and creativity.

Men and women who put their trust in the story of grace told in the Bible have more often than not been lights of imagination and love: Tolkien, C. S. Lewis (no intellectual slouches these two), Tolstoy, Solzhenitsyn, Mother Teresa and Wilberforce are just a few examples among millions of unnamed points of light.

In spite of those who have made the Bible a convenient whipping boy, I believe that after our culture has long crumbled into dust, its message will stand as the pinnacle of God's amazing sacrificial love and His unimpeachable wisdom.

But as much as I enjoy the Bible, there are still mysteries for me within its covers, ideas and interpretations about difficult passages that seem stretched and sketchy.

Frankly, it is not those thorny bits in the Bible that cause me the most problem. It is the parts that I understand with crystal clarity, the things that speak about what God desires and my less-than-sterling thoughts, motives and actions.

No wonder people use the pages of the Good Book just to press flowers and note births and deaths. If it is read and followed in earnest . . . well, who knows how one might end up?

Your word is a lamp to my feet and a light for my path.
Psalm 119:105, *NIV*

*The revelation of GOD is whole and pulls our lives together.
The signposts of GOD are clear and point out the right road. The
life-maps of GOD are right, showing the way to joy. The directions
of GOD are plain and easy on the eyes. GOD's reputation is
twenty-four-carat gold, with a lifetime guarantee. The decisions
of GOD are accurate down to the nth degree.*

Psalm 19:7-9, *THE MESSAGE*

12

THINKING IS CHRISTIAN

They stood at my door, sweating in their crisp white shirts, ties, dark slacks and leather shoes. There were two of them. Young and still pimply with adolescence, they could not see the irony in the name badge that identified them as "Elders."

After a greeting they proceeded with their script. One was the mouthpiece and the other the amen corner.

I was not interested in hearing their script and I told them so. I wanted to talk with *them* instead.

This threw the young men a bit, but they recovered and found another place in their script to continue from.

I asked them to reason with me; they gave me their testimony.

I asked them to think; they became flustered and gave me more party line.

I asked them to be intellectually honest; they more than subtly suggested that I was not listening to God.

We went way off the script, and the mouthpiece became agitated and combative while the quiet one suggested with his eyes that they abandon me as a lost cause.

I asked them to think, and they could not do it.

They had been well instructed on *what to think* and could not deviate from the playbook in spite of their quickly eroding position.

I felt very sorry for them as they stormed off. I knew they would write off our encounter as satanic oppression, with me being the tool of the devil to confuse them. (Sometimes it is fun to be the tool of the devil.)

These parrots were Mormons, of course, but in the way they refused to go off the party line script they could just as easily have been Christians.

I am not saying this to be mean, but to be honest; many Christians are busy teaching those under their care what to think, but we are not very good at teaching our people *how* to think. And I think this has a tendency to backfire on us.

At a certain point in life, teaching people how to reason, how to wrestle with varying thoughts and bring competing ideas to wise conclusions is essential for their spiritual growth—unless we are content to develop mimics.

I spent a number of decades working with teenagers and have owned four of them myself.

One observation that I found to ring true with kids who are mutating into adults is that at a certain point it is futile and even counterproductive to tell them *what to think*. (Especially when they hit that interesting time in life where they assume anything an adult says is probably dumb, and anything their moronic friend says is probably brilliant.)

This transition is particularly hard for parents to navigate. They are *used* to telling their kid what to think: eating the dog food is yucky, going to bed without brushing and flossing is disgusting, saying "thank you" is right and good, pushing other kids out of the way to get to the biggest piece is wrong.

And they are used to their kids nodding in at least some form of compliance.

I found with my own teens and with the countless others that I have helped pilot through adolescence, that while it was ineffective to tell them *what to think*, it was extremely helpful to teach them *how to think*.

This may seem like splitting hairs, but the two concepts are far different from each other.

A silly example might help.

Imagine that you were trying to instruct mice how to avoid a mousetrap. Holding up a picture of a mousetrap and saying, "Avoid this at all costs" would be teaching the mice what to think. The mice might effectively be conditioned to avoid any contraption that was made of wood, wires and cheese. But the fact is, there are a lot of really cool mousetraps being made that do not look or operate anything like the old-fashioned wood and wire types. A mouse would easily fall victim to one of those kinds of traps, and an instructor would have to work hard to keep his mice abreast of new developments in mousetraps.

On the other hand, if you wanted to teach your mice how to think, you would not need to go through the exercise of mouse-traps at all. Asking your mice to ponder the question, "Why would anyone want to lay cheese around for the taking?" would be getting the rodents to wrestle with the whole issue of traps and temptation for themselves.

Frankly, I think we Christians have done a very good job of teaching people about what mousetraps to avoid, but we have not helped them to understand why anyone would lay cheese around. And not just with kids, but with adults as well.

As I read the Gospels, it seems to me that the Pharisees were busy telling people what to think. They had all the answers, all the rules and the party line. Don't touch this, don't do that, wear this, eat that. Every issue was nicely tied up with a bow; they did all the thinking for you.

Jesus, on the other hand, forced thinking on people.

It was well known that if you went out to hear one of His sto-ries, the end result would be that you would leave scratching your head; and talking with others all the way home trying to figure out exactly what He was driving at. (Oh, would I LOVE to do that at church some Sunday morning!)

Much of what Jesus had to say was veiled, implied, mystical and symbolic.

The disciples, who undoubtedly heard the same stories and sayings repeated over and over again, had a tough time getting their minds around what He was trying to communicate and eventually slinked up to Him to beg for an explanation.

Even when Jesus was clear in what He said, He left a lot for us to sort out on our own.

For example, the general sense of the two big-league com-mands of God are obvious: love the Lord with all your heart, soul, mind and strength, and love your neighbor as you would yourself. But how that is done in everyday situations takes some real thinking.

Learning to think is a lot of work. It is much easier just to be told where the boundary lines are so we can start gauging our spiritual development by how well we stay within them. If we let people try to work things through in their own minds, they might come to conclusions different from ours (*gasp!*).

I was invited to be part of a VIP dinner at a conference I was speaking at. The room was filled with many of the bright lights of Christianity—authors, speakers, musicians.

I grabbed an open seat and soon found myself in a conversation with a young Christian author and activist. He was ranting (really, he was softly ranting at the dinner table) about politics, the poor, war, peace and all kinds of interesting things.

I disagreed with a whole bunch of what he said.

In polite company nowadays you should never let someone know you disagree with anything he or she says. Being naturally impolite (and the fact that he was ranting at the dinner table), I challenged his thinking on a particular issue.

The subject that we were talking about (which happened to be if there was ever a situation where a Christian was justified in using violent means to stop evil) was not as important as the essence of what we actually were doing. We were both putting our best argument out on that dinner table, in front of other good thinkers, not to score a point for our own genius but in order that we might live a life more in tune with the will of God.

Wrestling through the problem was a good exercise for both of us. It helped us see the strengths and perhaps the weaknesses of our own conclusions or even a need to modify or change how we thought about an area.

We left the dinner table as friends who disagreed but who were still processing.

It is far less work to just repeat a script that we have been given than to have to work out issues for ourselves. This error of the Pharisee crew has in large part been replicated in enough Christian churches that it has made us appear as programmed autotrons to those outside the faith.

Our unwillingness to be comfortable with the potential ambiguities that come when trying to work out how to live out the Christian life has created a problem for many Christians. Rather than struggle with Scripture, reason and real life, we settle for dogma built on a foundation with the strength of Jell-O.

The ambiguities can create some pretty interesting dialogues.

I created a weekend event especially designed to be attractive to men. It was located in a rustic, isolated mountain area. I made sure there was lots of terrific food and ample free time; I even hired masseurs to show up and give free massages. We set up a satellite dish to make sure we could show the Saturday game on a big screen. I hung more than a dozen hammocks in trees and had a well-stocked library of "guy" books available.

The men were enthused! It was a *Mantown*, and they felt right at home . . . so at home that one of the guys brought a cooler with a few beers in it and popped one open during the game.

Now some of the Christian men on this retreat became a bit agitated. A few had been raised to think that Jesus drank only grape juice and made a batch of Welch's at the wedding feast in Cana. Some were nervous for a couple of the guys who were recovering alcoholics. A few others asked if there was a spare beer.

Having neglected to mention anything about alcohol in my publicity for our weekend, I was in a quandary.

What exactly should I do or say . . . and to whom? Should I grab the beer away from the guy sucking on it because a few of the brethren held doctrinal positions that most of Christendom would view as loony and might take offense? (I should point out that the beer drinker came from a Lutheran family who, like their founder, saw beer drinking almost as a sacrament.)

Should I shush those who were teetotalers by quoting Paul's admonition to "drink a little wine for the sake of your stomach" (see 1 Tim. 5:23)? What exactly does the Bible say about having a beer (not half a dozen beers, but one beer) while watching a football game with your brothers? Where did the law of love and the law of liberty connect, overlap or overrule?

Maybe the answer is easy for you. It wasn't for me. (And I don't even drink.)

So I did nothing.

I just told people who had a concern to talk about it with the other men. I think it was a good exercise.

And I am planning another men's gathering, but I haven't decided yet if I should say anything about bringing beer.

I hope this got you thinking.

> *When I was a child, I talked like a child, I thought like*
> *a child, I reasoned like a child. When I became a man,*
> *I put childish ways behind me.*
>
> 1 Corinthians 13:11, *NIV*

> *You're blessed when you meet Lady Wisdom, when you make*
> *friends with Madame Insight. She's worth far more than money*
> *in the bank; her friendship is better than a big salary. Her value*
> *exceeds all the trappings of wealth; nothing you could wish for*
> *holds a candle to her. With one hand she gives long life, with the*
> *other she confers recognition. Her manner is beautiful, her life*
> *wonderfully complete. She's the very Tree of Life to those who*
> *embrace her. Hold her tight—and be blessed!*
>
> Proverbs 3:13-18, *THE MESSAGE*

> *I will instruct you and teach you in the way you should go; I will*
> *counsel you and watch over you. Do not be like the horse or the*
> *mule, which have no understanding but must be controlled by*
> *bit and bridle or they will not come to you.*
>
> Psalm 32:8-9, *NIV*

13

DOING SOMETHING
BIG FOR GOD

"I want to do something big for God," he said. And he meant it. A bright, hard charger with a verbal gift, there was no doubt in my mind that whatever he touched would flower.

I have to admit, I like this kind of people.

They build a skyscraper rather than a home; they can see what could be rather than what is. They are big thinkers with a finger on the pulse of the world they live in and a faith in possibilities that would freeze the average man in his tracks. They seem to have no fear of failure, even on a massive scale. They are energizing to be around.

These are the people that often end up with the mega churches, the radio shows, the big book sales and, eventually, the agents and bodyguards. They are the speakers who can draw in the crowd, the movers and shakers who are at the forefront of the action. They have admirers, critics and even disciples. Google their name and the monitor screen instantly fills up. In short, they are successful. And most of us are attracted to people whose lives seem triumphant.

The majority of us, I think, secretly desire to make a successful impact with our lives. I can't recall one person I have known who expressed the hope to grow up to be mediocre or aspired to be a complete and utter failure. No potential writer hopes that his or her book will sell only a few hundred copies; no expectant actor is pleased at the idea of his or her effort going straight into a bargain bin. Nobody wants to create a business that goes bust, or make a product nobody wants.

Of course, believers with their heads screwed on straight hope that their lives will count for something big, in an eternal sense.

We may not all want to dwell in the national spotlight, but most of us long for significance. We hope that whatever we put our hearts and hand to flourishes.

And this, I believe, is not just human vanity or an impulse from the more diabolical part of our soul. I truly believe we have been hardwired by our Creator to make a difference, not only in the temporal world with our buildings, inventions, talents, art and ideas, but in the eternal world as well.

But the fact is, most of us don't think we have done much that is significant, especially if we start comparing our lives with the big shots we know, read about or see on television.

One time I was checking into a hotel when an entire pro football team came rolling into the foyer. The mass, girth and collective power of these men made me quite aware of my insufficiency as a male. Without a word spoken, I was reduced to Walter Mitty status, at least in my mind.

Get around a few people with *real* accomplishments and see how a contribution such as "I drive middle school kids home every Wednesday night" measures up to what they have done or are doing. If we live in the shadow of an overachiever, particularly a spiritual one, it can make us feel quite inadequate.

But this is where the mystery begins.

Not everything is as it seems. What looks like success to us may produce a boring yawn from God, and what seems inconsequential may be something that will be celebrated forever.

One often does not know what chain of events a simple act of obedience to the whisper of God will produce. And it is in the obedience to that whisper that significance and eternal meaning are usually found.

My friend Ed is a smiling, friendly house painter. He went through some tough ground before coming to Christ—divorce and single fatherhood after the untimely death of his ex-wife, to name a few hurdles. As his Christian faith grew, he attempted to honor God with what resources he had, particularly his painting skill and labor.

When we were constructing a new church campus, Ed almost single-handedly painted the whole thing. And few knew that he had done it; they just showed up and remarked how nice every-thing looked.

For a guy who was never going to be on the radio, write a book, hit the mission field or deliver a sermon, painting the church buildings was pretty big, and I am sure God is honored by his ef-forts. I know it is to His honor that the place we meet together is attractive and not ratty looking.

But when it came to doing big things for God, painting the church was not it. The big thing came unannounced, unplanned and could have been easily missed.

Ed was driving home from town. Ahead on the side of the road stood a diminutive older man, white hair, small white mustache. He had his thumb out.

Now Ed, for all of his kindness, is not the type of person who picks up just anyone hitching for a ride; yet as the distance closed between Ed and the hitchhiker, a quiet sense not yet even a whis-per said, "Pick this man up."

Ed had a thousand reasons why it was impractical to stop for a hitchhiker at that moment, but the voice inside of him deepened and strengthened: *Pick this man up.*

Ed pulled off the road. He didn't know that the older man to whom he opted to give a lift was a man who was virtually at the end of himself: a Vietnam vet, an alcoholic, a man whose relation-ships had all ended in colossal train wrecks.

"Where you headed?" asked Ed as the man entered the car.

The small town that he said was his destination was at least 20 minutes past Ed's turnoff. Yet something impressed him to not drop the man off on the side of the road; so Ed said, "Well, that's a little outta my way, but I can take you there."

"Thanks, I appreciate it," said the stranger in a voice gravelly and smoke-tinged as an ashtray.

It turned out that Ed and the hitchhiker shared the same first name, and for reasons unknown, the older man decided that this stranger was someone he could reveal his burdened soul to.

Ed had never shared Christ with someone, and by his own ad-mission, he didn't do such a terrific job explaining God's love to the stranger in his truck. But whatever he said prompted the older man to ask if it was okay if he could come to church sometime.

By the time Ed let the old hitchhiker off at the public assistance apartments where he lived, it had been arranged that Ed would pick him up on Sunday morning.

And so it was that Sunday after Sunday, Ed and the man many of us would simply refer to as Old Ed would arrive together and leave together.

For Old Ed, it only took one encounter with the gospel to turn his heart to Christ and begin restoring the life that he had frittered away. Within a few months, Old Ed had shared about his new life in Christ with everyone in his apartment complex. Every Sunday morning finds him on a front row seat with a clear mind and joyous smile.

I think my friend Ed did something big for God that day he picked up a hitchhiker; something bigger than writing a best-selling book or getting on a radio program; something bigger than inventing a car engine that runs on water, or even single-handedly painting a whole church.

And the beauty of it was that it is nothing Ed could have foreseen, prepared for or made to happen. He was simply responding to the prompting of the Holy Spirit to pull over and take this old man with his thumb out to his home.

Ed still marvels at how God used him, made the right words come out even though he thought he was gargling marbles, gave him love for a stranger and acted as a conduit to see a life changed.

I sometimes think that we have the whole big thing for God all upside down. We create celebrities out of authors who have sold lots of books, or out of pastors who have huge churches, as if God was impressed with them as well or they have some secret and inside track to spirituality.

I know some of these kinds of people, and I must tell you that they won't be the ones sitting by my bedside when I am in a world of hurt. They are much too busy doing big things for God.

I think the biggest thing we can do for God is to just listen to His whisper, to simply obey His order to pull the car over and pick up the old man with his thumb out. To listen when He says to give a little extra cash to someone, to respond when He prods us to volunteer to help or tell someone the story of our faith.

These are seeds of obedience. They are planted and often forgotten during our journey. But we may someday find that those seemingly insignificant seeds have grown to be the biggest trees in the heavenly forest, while the big-deal people out there with the big plans and big publicity only end up with spiritual shrubs.

Now all has been heard; here is the conclusion of the matter: Fear God and keep his commandments, for this is the whole duty of man.

Ecclesiastes 12:13, *NIV*

As Jesus was saying these things, a woman in the crowd called out, "Blessed is the mother who gave you birth and nursed you." He replied, "Blessed rather are those who hear the word of God and obey it."

Luke 11:27-28, *NIV*

The LORD said, "Go out and stand on the mountain in the presence of the LORD, for the LORD is about to pass by." Then a great and powerful wind tore the mountains apart and shattered the rocks before the LORD, but the LORD was not in the wind. After the wind there was an earthquake, but the LORD was not in the earthquake. After the earthquake came a fire, but the LORD was not in the fire. And after the fire came a gentle whisper.

1 Kings 19:11-13, *NIV*

14

THE WHIPPING BOY*

His hands were sunk deep into his pockets and he made very little eye contact as he explained to me why I hadn't seen him around church for a while.

It seems that the "church" had let him down in some way. He was disappointed with the way that a touchy situation was handled.

His gripe wasn't with everybody. In fact, most of the congregation didn't have a clue as to the issue that turned into the proverbial last straw. The whole congregation had not lined up to corporately kick him in the head. In reality, it was a couple of fellow church members who had committed the foul that soured him on us all.

"They weren't speaking for me," I assured him.

"I know," he replied and then shrugged as if to say, "Too bad, but I now have a reason to bail out."

I have to admit, I felt somewhat hurt and disappointed, and I guess it reflected on my face.

"I haven't gone to another church," he said, as if that would be reassuring. "I sorta don't go anywhere right now."

Yeah, that solution is much better, I thought sarcastically to myself. But I kept my mouth shut so as not to be added to the *mean people of the church* list he had started.

I don't know why, but I have a hard time not taking it personally when somebody who has a bit of history with our community of faith decides to part company, especially over something that is fairly trivial or because of the actions or poor choices of a few individuals.

---

* A **whipping boy**, in feudal times, was a boy of the same age but lower rank raised with a prince or nobleman as a playmate, who was whipped in his place when the young nobleman—too high in standing to be beaten by anyone below his father, who was often unavailable—misbehaved or slacked in his studies.

If you listen to people who have broken away from a Christian community or who are plotting their exit strategy, their words flog the same carcass: the crummy church.

The crummy church, all they want is your money!

The crummy church, nobody is friendly.

The crummy church, someone is trying to boss you around and always trying to tell you what to do.

The crummy church, overflowing with hypocrites!

The crummy church fails to recognize and thank me for my very important contributions.

The crummy church is the convenient whipping boy for their dissatisfaction.

At the risk of being cynical, I believe that I should point out that many times the people who whip the church are really making revealing comments about their own failings and shortcomings.

The guy who thinks the church wants his money is often the person who is tightfisted and consumed with the pursuit of the dollar.

The one who gripes about the unfriendliness of others often is the same person who slips into a corner seat, runs for the door at the end of worship and never says a warm "hello" to anyone else.

The hypocrite spotters are often the ones so conscious of their own hypocrisies being exposed that they quickly can find it in others.

The one who thinks the church is unthankful often is the one who has no idea of what it means to be a servant and often gets failing grades for his or her own affirmations.

I think Jesus had these kinds of people in mind when He humorously suggested that some people complain about the specks in others' eyes while entertaining a piece of lumber in their own.

Yet it is true that sometimes we believers can be a cantankerous and rotten lot.

I have been part of church congregations long enough to know that there can be some very strange and even terribly ungodly behavior erupting from within them from time to time.

I still recall a church that employed me for a raucous time as their middle school youth pastor descending into absolute insanity shortly after I had moved on. It got so bad that one morning a troublemaking member of the church decided to stage a rebellion over the choice of a new pastor by closing the place down. The rebel went around chaining and padlocking shut the entry doors very early on a Sunday morning.

As you can imagine, this put a kink in the worship service that day.

There is no question that some church communities have lost their way, and to stick around and hope that somehow things will get better is an exercise in futility. And I have no doubt that some churches actually need to be abandoned before they sink into the icy waters of heresy, abuse or plain old nuttiness.

Some churches have leaders who are power hungry, immature, foolish or even immoral, and their out-of-whack leadership creates strife, confusion and pain.

I have witnessed smaller Christian communities that are merely the domain of one or two families who make sure that their dynasty is never threatened by newcomers, hired pastors or God Himself.

From time to time you find a group of Christian people who, in practical terms, no longer have Jesus as the core of what they are about. Some worship their building, some their doctrine, some their distinctions, some their history.

Some groups are so paralyzed by their own policies and rules that they have frozen into an institution instead of a living, organic and, at times, spiritually unruly organism fueled by the Holy Spirit.

But while any group of people may have a few warts of these kinds, the vast majority of Christian communities are generally sane, workable folks who, like the rest of us, imperfectly seek to honor God. The Christian churches that have obviously gone off the rails, well, these are the exceptions, not the rule.

Most churches bump along without a major scandal or crisis for years on end. Most of them are not hotbeds of looniness.

One thing that all these truly Christian churches have in common is that they are made up of people. And you can count on the fact that people, if you hang around them long enough, will let you down, make a bad call or give you a swift elbow to the head.

Every pastor or leader I know has a weak spot (actually, maybe a number of weak spots) or makes a faulty decision now and then.

Every person in every community of faith that I have ever been a part of has a chink in their armor or is guilty, at times, of poor judgment—without exception.

Every Christian I have spent any time with has sometimes lost his or her focus, objectivity, discipline and, on occasion, faith.

You see, when people in our community of faith talk negatively about the church, they are not talking about the building we meet in or some iconic institution; they are talking about me, about my friends, about my brothers and sisters.

They are saying that I let them down. They are saying that I want their money. They are saying that I am unfriendly. They are saying that I want to boss them around. They are saying that I am a hypocrite. They are saying that I don't care about them. They are saying that I am the reason they are dissatisfied, restless or ready to break ties.

Because, I am the church, and my believing friends are the church, elbows and all.

Those believers who have done some interesting mental math that allows them to abandon the rest of us and spend Sunday mornings sleeping in, washing the car or going fishing, well, they are the church too. They belong to us even if they want to heave rocks in our direction or flog us as they try to explain why every church has let them down or is unworthy of their participation.

To have a whipping boy is convenient. Using the church as whipping boy seems impersonal and therefore takes the smacks and backhanded comments, which in many cases are from the personal frustrations, failures and shortcomings that we can't muster the courage or ability to deal with in a godly way.

However, when whipping on the church, one must be very, very careful. We are getting into family sensitivities here. And this family is covered by powerful protection. When we go after the church in a critical way, spewing venom and disdain, we are actually scooting out on some very thin and dangerous ice. For we are insulting someone very near and dear to Jesus, someone He will protect at all costs. Someone He gave his life for: His bride, the church.

> *Built on the foundation of the apostles and prophets,*
> *with Christ Jesus himself as the chief cornerstone. In him the*
> *whole building is joined together and rises to become a holy*
> *temple in the Lord. And in him you too are being built together*
> *to become a dwelling in which God lives by his Spirit.*
>
> Ephesians 2:20-22, *NIV*

> *Christ loved the church and gave himself up for her to make her*
> *holy, cleansing her by the washing with water through the word,*
> *and to present her to himself as a radiant church, without stain*
> *or wrinkle or any other blemish, but holy and blameless.*
>
> Ephesians 5:26-27, *NIV*

15

COSMIC HUMOR AT MY EXPENSE

One of the things I learned early in my Christian experience was to never tell God that you are willing to do whatever He wants or go wherever He pleases . . . *except* _____ (fill in the blank: become a missionary in the Congo, be a pastor's wife, work with old people, homosexuals, mentally challenged, homeless, and so on).

The reason is obvious if you have cruised around Christians for a while. It seems, at least from the testimonies you hear, that God gets His cosmic jollies by putting people who offer their lives to Him exactly where they don't want to be. And then to add insult to injury, He actually makes them *appreciate* it.

That little word "except" gets them in trouble every time. And it seems to happen so consistently that I would swear it is part of God's routine.

He may even find it funny: *Ah ha! There is another mortal trying to hedge his bets and offer Me his life at the same time. That kid is a ball of prejudice and self-importance and doesn't even know it. I think I'll send him to work in the inner city without a Ghetto Pass; that oughta grind off those rough edges in a hurry! Ha, ha, ha.*

Take a brief tour of the Bible and you will often find the cosmic humor I am describing at work.

Consider Moses.

The *last place* in the world he wanted to see again was Egypt. A wanted man with bad memories of the land of the pharaohs, he had settled down happily and far away with a wife and a bunch of sheep.

Then God shows up, lighting bushes on fire, making snakes out of staffs, and not taking any excuses. He sends Moses packing back to Egypt, no doubt grumbling in a stutter to his brother, Aaron, who was drafted as well and wondering how he got in the middle of this mess.

Ha! Ha! Ha!

God doesn't even ask permission before He rearranges your plans.

A quick study, I figured out this trap door in the eschatological universe. My first thought was to see if I could work the system. And learning something from Br'er Rabbit, I thought it would be much safer to tell God *not* to throw me in the Br'er Patch.

You see, I wanted to move to Hawaii.

I had fallen in love with the slow-paced life on one of the outer islands. I wanted to surf the perfect waves in the clear water without a wetsuit; go without shoes every day; have my children experience a rural life, mixed culture, extended family (called Ohana); live without air conditioning or heating and be able to leave my front door unlocked and the keys in my car (car theft being sort of pointless on a small island . . . just stand at Walmart and pretty soon your car will drive by).

"Please, God, whatever You do, please, never, never send me to serve You in Hawaii, especially on that miserably beautiful and surf-filled island of Kauai" would be my prayer.

But, of course, God would see through that ploy right away, so I just decided to move to Hawaii. Then through gritted teeth, I told God that He had my reluctant permission to change the direction of my compass and I waited for the probable outcome, assuming that I would end up in North Dakota. All the while the angels would laugh out loud at the cosmic joke of sending a born-and-bred surf guy about as far from the ocean as one could get.

Going on several decades of living in the land of trade winds has made me realize that sometimes our desires and God's desires for us are actually in cahoots. (But I am still willing to go to North Dakota if He really, really wants me to. Unenthusiastically willing, I might add.)

I have a sneaking suspicion that God knows I would be pretty worthless to Him languishing in the Midwest. He knows He is dealing with defective goods.

But this doesn't mean that God isn't going to initiate a little cosmic humor at our expense just because we have dodged the "Please don't send me to the Congo" bullet. Rough edges have to be ground off, and His methods are sometimes so blatant that even the victims have to stop and chuckle.

As careful as I am about what to pray for or what to attempt to dictate to God here and there, I still become a player in God's comedy script. The latest was what happened with Jim.

Now, in my own defense, I must tell you that I pretty much like everybody and I assume that most people like me. You have to work very hard to get on my blacklist, and it is a very short list. I have a high tolerance for knuckleheads, oddballs and kooks of every sort. There are very few people that I just can't take being around.

But Jim was one of those people.

A grown-up man with a wife and kids, Jim was just flat-out obnoxious.

His wife and children attended our church, but Jim didn't have any use for God. A fairy tale, a crutch, a myth for morons was how he saw our faith.

I would bump into Jim at the beach now and then.

He liked to talk.

Boy, did he like to talk.

But talking to him was similar to talking to a 14-year-old with ADD who had spent too much time looking at naked lady pictures.

His language was filthy, the f-bomb his primary adjective, noun and verb. The subject matter was always the same: how drunk he had gotten, how insane he was surfing or the equipment displayed on the nearest female.

There was no sense of propriety, no sense that he was speaking to a Christian (much less a pastor) who might not be interested in his latest excessive adventure; no sense that he was broadcasting these things in a public setting, around kids and families.

Rude subject matter, which might occasionally slip in when in dialogue with an unbelieving rogue, was a constant with Jim.

He wouldn't let me get away. He couldn't read the dull look in my eyes or my obvious lack of enthusiasm for most of the subject matter. It got to the point that if I saw him coming, I would try to slip through the bushes, engage in another conversation or make myself scarce in one way or another.

I would imagine that all of us have our own version of "Jim."

Perhaps it is the constant complainer, the perennial gossip, the pinheaded officemate or the crotchety neighbor. Maybe it is the swishy gay guy who wants to see if he can incite the hellfire and damnation he knows is right under the surface of every Christian. Perhaps it is the über-liberal or hyper-conservative. Maybe the guy who gets you riled up is the one who wants all of us to join his tree-hugging bandwagon, or the capitalist agitating to have you join the gang who want to clear-cut the Amazon. There is someone out there to drive even the best of us crazy.

We plaster on our fake Christian smile when we see them coming our way and try to pretend we are somewhat interested in their banal little life. While most other people just put an end to the farce and act rude to their tormentors, we Christians have to put up with it, bear the burden, remind ourselves that Jesus died for them, too, and talk ourselves into hanging on for a few more minutes of torture.

I was clearly at that spot with Jim. I came out from behind my Christian mask and shared my disdain for Jim with my wife.

"I just can't stand the guy," I told her. "I keep hoping that God will give me patience, but I am sorry, he is one person I am having a real hard time wanting to show any grace to."

My wife was empathetic. She has a few of those people in the orbit of her life as well.

Two days later the phone rang.

It was Jim. He was upset, frantic. Did I have any time to talk?

I spent the morning sitting on the steps of a construction trailer with Jim. He was a broken man. His philandering had caught up with him. His wife was done with him, his family fractured.

Stuff was coming out of his mouth that I never thought I would hear. He cursed his pride and his foolishness; and with language laced with every obscenity known to man, he bemoaned his sin.

I invited Jim to accept the forgiveness offered by the cross and turn his mismanaged life over to Jesus.

On his trailer steps he prayed with me and put his faith in Christ.

Tears flowed—his and mine.

The rest of the day was surreal.

"Guess whom I prayed with today to become a Christian?" I asked my wife when she came home from work.

She couldn't guess and about fell over when I told her.

In the passing months Jim became a friend.

I laugh privately at the fact that his heart has changed faster than his language; and hearing him tell me, using words that would scorch a sailor, how Jesus took a person like him and gave him a new life is a hoot.

He has gobbled down the Bible, C. S. Lewis's *Mere Christianity* and *The Great Divorce*, and J. I. Packer's *Knowing God* . . . for starters.

It turned out that Jim was not the mindless hedonist he had made himself out to be, but an intelligent, sensitive man who was just very, very lost.

We get together a couple of times a week, and at our last meeting, Jim pulled out of a notebook in which he journals about his faith—a song, a hymn really—deep, personal and full of awe and glory to God.

It was something on a par with any psalm.

His wife is stunned at the change in the man. Their marriage is being glued back together.

"I wrote a song for my wife, too," Jim told me. "It is private, but I'll let you read it," he said.

The song was a beautiful poem of love for a woman who had the courage to take back a man who had hurt her so grievously. While they are not divorced, it ended by his asking her to marry him again.

I leaned back in my chair, Jim's beaming face across from me and his words of gratitude and love in my hands.

And I thought I heard something: laughter from the cosmos, laughing at me, laughing at Jim, laughing at the divine irony that was taking place.

Ha! Ha! Ha!

> *On hearing this, Jesus said to them, "It is not the healthy*
> *who need a doctor, but the sick. I have not come to call*
> *the righteous, but sinners."*

Mark 2:17, *NIV*

> *I tell you that in the same way there will be more rejoicing*
> *in heaven over one sinner who repents than over*
> *ninety-nine righteous persons who do not need to repent.*

Luke 15:7, *NIV*

16

THE ESCALATOR

"They should know better!" she said sternly. The others around the table nodded in apparent approval of this judgment.

Normally, I would have been among the nodders, for there is a perverse bit of fun in being able to see, evaluate and be the umpire for the actions of others.

But for some reason, this day I didn't join in the fun. Instead, the statement unleashed a bunny trail of thought, which I immediately decided to hop down.

I remembered a time long before 9-11 crimped down our borders when I managed to haul several dozen kids from a poverty ridden orphanage outside of Tijuana, Mexico, to an affluent part of Southern California for a weekend splurge of their little lifetime.

I recalled that we had just come from a shoe store where, thanks to the generosity of folks in the church, each child had been allowed to actually pick any pair of new shoes that struck their fancy—a new and novel experience for them all.

For a chaotic 45 minutes the kids went wild with the miracle of free choice and massive selection. Few had ever owned anything but very well-used, thin-treaded shoes dropped off at the orphanage as donations.

We took the kids with their crispy new shoes to a well-manicured local park in order to break in the footwear and enjoy a massive lunch, which some kind ladies had provided.

One little kid, a scrawny eight-year-old named Roberto, had just finished plowing through a small bag of potato chips. Licking the salt off his lips he nonchalantly crumpled the bag and tossed it on the grass.

Seeing the desecration to this well-kept public park, I strolled over and called Roberto back to the scene of the crime. In my best high school Spanish I directed him to pick up his litter and then walked him over to one of the plentiful trash cans where, as is the case in California, there was plastered a warning against littering and the resultant fine, in *both* the English and Spanish language.

After he deposited his empty chip bag into the yawning mouth of the trash can, I pointed out the signage to him and read it to him in the Spanish version, emphasizing the part about a $150 fine for violators.

The little kid stared at the sign and then stared back at me for a moment. Then, shaking his little head, he looked up at me and said, "I'm glad I live in Mexico where it is free!"

After this pronouncement, the kid skipped off to join his friends who were losing their lunch on the manually pushed little carousel.

I stood next to the trashcan thunderstruck.

I had been raised to understand that putting litter into trash receptacles was a sign of responsibility, good manners, consideration and social awareness. It never crossed my mind that anyone could translate such an obvious necessity of civilized life as a sign of a police state.

Roberto had been raised in such a way that the idea that someone would actually fine you for tossing your trash on the ground was akin to Gestapo tactics and the reduction of freedom.

"He should have known better."

But how?

Is an abhorrence of littering a moral value that is written on the heart, or hard-wired into the soul?

Blowing trash around the barren orphanage where he lived was as common and familiar as manicured lawns in Southern California. In his mind, maybe we were the strange ones, putting all that energy, money and time into keeping our grass clipped and leaves picked up.

But to be honest, I am constantly frustrated by people who "should have known better." And indeed, even a person raised in a moral cesspool certainly knows that you shouldn't steal, lie, cheat, fold, spindle or mutilate.

I think.

I do know that it would never occur to my children to send thank-you notes for kindnesses, gifts or money they have received if my wife had not strapped them to a chair and made it darn clear that they would fulfill this obligation before they would be allowed to escape outdoors to play.

Our hope is that by the time they are 30 or 40 years old, acknowledging the kindness of others will be part of their character.

The conversation around the table that had drawn me back to the small adventure in the park had moved on by the time I returned from my bunny trail of thought, but the essence of this problem stayed with me.

You see, I serve as a pastor to a congregation that is made up of a strange mix of people: those who *know better* and people who *ought to know better* but don't seem to.

The "ought to know better" people often frustrate the "people who know better."

The problem I have is that I am not always sure that the people who ought to know better *really do know better* or, like little Roberto, they don't have a clue of the right way to act, even if propriety seems obvious to the others around them.

The gal who lives with her boyfriend rather than marry him so that she doesn't lose her welfare benefits ought to know better.

The real estate agent who maneuvers things in such a way that he steals the client of another agent ought to know better.

The quirky loner who once in a while digs out a joint and smokes it by himself in the backyard ought to know better.

The business traveler who flips the hotel TV to the X-rated channel while away from wife and family ought to know better.

Perhaps they do.

I would.

But then I have been a believer for a long while now and have had a long time to process the nuances of the faith and how they apply to everyday living situations.

I am also not on welfare or in a dog-eat-dog business. And I am not always on the road, nor am I a quirky loner.

It is not good enough to huff "Well, if they read their Bibles . . ." because many of them do, and for reasons known only to God, the Holy Spirit has not illuminated the concept in their hearts even though the principle seems to be quite obvious.

Nor is it a problem that Christian values are not being taught . . . they are, but like a customer at a smorgasbord, it seems that a lot of Christian people pick and choose what seems appetizing to them within Christianity. Or perhaps a more apt example may be that we are like little children who refuse to eat fare that we will some day develop a taste for.

The bigger and far more important question is, *what do we do* with someone who ought to know better?

A few years ago, I went on a surf adventure to Samoa with a dozen guys from our church. It was a wonderful time of new surf spots and exploring a small, undeveloped island where the culture, habits and way of life were significantly different from what we were used to.

Upon returning to the United States, we landed in Honolulu and proceeded with other fellow travelers, who were mostly non-U.S. citizens, through the maze that leads to customs and immigration.

At the end of a corridor there was a single escalator that led to the main customs area; and traffic was backed up.

There at the base of the escalator was an old Samoan woman traveling alone. Her foot pawed in the air but she would not place it on the erupting steel steps of the escalator.

It was quite obvious that this old lady was in the midst of a new and unnavigable experience. Her whole life had been spent in the small single-level dwellings of Samoa, and any second-story exposure had been reached by steps, not an escalator.

But the travel-weary crowd was patient, sympathetic even. As the old woman tried to find her rhythm on the escaping steps, she would lift her foot and almost place it down only to react fearfully and replant it on the ground to study the situation anew.

I think that many had compassion for her. For this little old lady, jumping onto a moving set of stairs must have been like asking the rest of us to mount a bucking bronco.

So we waited, hoping that she would figure it out so that all of us could get on with declaring what we had in our luggage and finally get home.

The line was getting longer and people in the far back who couldn't witness the drama were now grumbling.

The little old lady pawed away, but there was fear in her eyes. It was obvious that she was in a situation beyond her ability.

Then two of the guys from the surf trip stepped up to the old woman and gently took her arms.

She was small and frail enough that they almost lifted her off the ground as they placed her on the rising stairs and then snuggled in close enough so that she knew she could not fall.

Some people applauded, and more than a few chuckled.

It seems to me that perhaps this is the way we should treat those who ought to know better.

Rather than gripe about the fact that the task in front of them is so obvious and intuitive (which actually may be debatable), perhaps what we need to do is simply move close enough to them to lovingly carry them toward the goal.

We carry them by praying for them. We carry them by taking the time to hear their story. We carry them by offering grace and patience so that they can learn the rhythm of the Christian walk. We carry them by getting close enough that our love lifts them to a place their own abilities and understanding can't take them.

Of course it is much easier to complain, to throw a few stones of criticism and readjust our judge's robe.

But then we know better . . . don't we?

My conscience is clear, but that does not make me innocent.
It is the Lord who judges me. Therefore judge nothing before the
appointed time; wait till the Lord comes. He will bring to light
what is hidden in darkness and will expose the motives of men's
hearts. At that time each will receive his praise from God.

1 Corinthians 4:4-5, *NIV*

17

THE RICHEST MAN

There is nothing like a cocky novice.

The hotshot beginner who thinks he knows how to drive on mud, ice or sand and ends up on his knees, digging his car out.

The "I can handle . . ." boasting kook who paddles out to a surf spot past his ability level and ends up doing the rock dance while picking up pieces of his surfboard.

The gullible girl who truly believes, in spite of all warnings to the contrary, that the 20-year-old slacker who delivers pizza to her family is the man of her dreams.

During World War II, it was the cocky replacements coming in with saber-rattling bravado and big boasts about how they were going to teach the Nazis a lesson that were slaughtered quickly. The veterans of battle, the men who had everything to teach, usually never even bothered to learn the names of these new men. Those who had experienced the horror of battle knew that it took more than mere bluster to survive; it took studied learning on the battlefield and more than a bit of luck.

Many seasoned guys can look back at some of the stupid stunts they did and idiotic moves they made in their younger years and marvel that they are still in one piece or not in jail.

Of course young men and women think they are invincible and unbreakable. Death and disaster are reserved for the old, the stupid or those intentionally trying to win the Darwin Award.

Those of us with some life mileage under our belts remember how it was.

We were too in control to end up addicted; too fast and flexible to get hurt; too shrewd to be ripped off; too brilliant to read the instructions; and too smart to seek out the advice of those who had the very experience we needed to learn from. We were exceptions to the rule of good sense . . . who often ended up as "let that be a lesson" illustrations of what that meant.

It is the very nature of being young to feel above and beyond what can only be learned from experience. But there is something else lurking in the back of every young skull that propels this cavalier, know-it-all attitude; it is pride.

Whether it is because of wisdom gained, the passing of physical prime, the fact that I have a family or the combination of all of the above, I have lost my insane desire to surf giant waves or go back to riding reservoir walls on a skateboard.

I am quicker to read the instructions before I put the thing together, and map out driving directions before getting in the car and "just going." But that darn kernel of pride is still difficult to quash.

Pride can outlast our ability to really hurt ourselves.

I know plenty of guys long past their idiot days of whom others say with exasperation under their breath, "Good grief, you can't teach that guy anything!"

And typically, the people who "know it all" also seem to have a series of disasters on their hands (but never their fault, mind you). They are fired from jobs, have their marriages implode, create riffs and divisions, and have financial failures or a series of aborted businesses.

At first glance this seems to be a man's disease. After all, guys are the ones who refuse to stop and ask for directions, peek at the car manual, read self-help books or seek financial counsel.

But women can be stubborn learners, too, and know quite well how to flex that little muscle of feminine pride.

A great irony is that some people are even proud of their hardheaded pride. "At least I did it my way!" they boast, as if self-designing your own train wreck was something you ought to get a medal for.

This is a strange tendency—avoiding wisdom, instruction and learning from those who clearly have something of value to offer. It permeates all levels of the human race.

More baffling than those who don't have insight are those who seek wisdom from people who are equally clueless or even failures in the very area in which they seek wisdom. For example: asking wisdom about marriage from a person who has repeatedly screwed up his or her marriage; talking business with a person who can't find two nickels to rub together; listening to spiritual non-sense from a clown who is . . . uh, um, "doctrinally challenged."

I find this kernel of pride trying to take root in me over and over again. More times than I can count I have made a summary judgment that some person had nothing to offer me that I didn't already know. Typically, the end result once I got around to listening to him or her was to be humbled at how much I ended up learning from this person and kicking myself for not paying attention to that wisdom much sooner.

I sometimes wonder how many blessings I have missed because the only counsel I wanted to listen to was my own.

Repeatedly over the years, I have made a wrong assumption because I never bothered to get all the facts and acted when I should have studied and prayed, rushed to judgment without considering all the evidence and found myself in that difficult place of having to try to back out of a bad move.

I have a sneaking suspicion that I am not alone here.

There are voices crying in the wilderness of our stupidity. There are people who are really trying to help the novices make wise choices, godly mathematicians who can demonstrate from Scripture and example the predictable equations of the kingdom of God.

I have a friend who tries to do this with the young people in our church who are graduating from high school. I call him "Doc."

Doc has been very successful and smart in his life choices, especially in his financial dealings. I knew he had not come from a moneyed family, and he had put himself through medical school by sacrifice, discipline, ingenuity and working hard after school hours and studies.

In contrast to his background, he has managed to create what is commonly referred to as a "comfortable" life for his family.

One day he explained to me the turning point for him.

Doc, a bright but rowdy high school student, was about to graduate when a wealthy friend of the family came to him with a graduation present. It was a book, old even at that time, of parable-like stories called *The Richest Man in Babylon*. The older man put the book in his hand and told him that the wisdom he had drawn from this book about dealing with money had been the secret to his wealth.

Even though it was loaded with "thees" and "thous" in its dialogue, Doc was intrigued, and he took the book and read it from cover to cover, digesting the commonsense principles in it.

"It changed how I thought about handling finances," Doc said to me with a smile. "And do you know what? Every year at graduation time, this is the book that I give to kids of family friends who are about to go on to college. On the inside cover I tell the little story of how I was given this same book upon my graduation and how it made all the difference in the world about how I dealt with money."

There was a twinkle in his eye and a pause in his story.

"Oh, and I've written a generous check to them and inserted it two-thirds of the way in the book."

I could see it in my mind.

The young graduate going through the cards and gifts, greedily scooping up the cash, comes upon a book with an odd title.

Must be some kind of Bible story book or something, the kid thinks, maybe even a bit miffed that this was the best Doc and his family could do for him, and then tosses it aside to deal with another day, not knowing the worth of the thing he has so casually discarded. Then, one boring rainy day, he picks up the book and it draws him in. And there, as the wisdom of stewardship floods upon him, he finds the hidden gift.

"That's a pretty cool idea," I said.

"You wanna know something else?" Doc asked.

"Sure!" I replied.

He twisted up an ironic smile and leaned forward and softly said, "I've been doing this for years, and as of yet, I've not had one check cashed."

Good friend, take to heart what I'm telling you; collect my counsels and guard them with your life. Tune your ears to the world of Wisdom; set your heart on a life of Understanding.

*That's right—if you make Insight your priority, and won't
take no for an answer, searching for it like a prospector panning
for gold, like an adventurer on a treasure hunt, believe me,
before you know it Fear-of-GOD will be yours; you'll have come
upon the Knowledge of God. And here's why: GOD gives out
Wisdom free, is plainspoken in Knowledge and Understanding.
He's a rich mine of Common Sense for those who live well,
a personal bodyguard to the candid and sincere. He keeps his eye
on all who live honestly, and pays special attention to his loyally
committed ones. So now you can pick out what's true and fair,
find all the good trails! Lady Wisdom will be your close friend,
and Brother Knowledge your pleasant companion. Good Sense
will scout ahead for danger, Insight will keep an eye out for you.*

Proverbs 2:1-11, *THE MESSAGE*

18

IN PIECES

Saint Francis of Assisi had a nickname for his own body; he called it "Brother Donkey."

I have always liked that image.

The spiritual or intellectual part of us says to do something—get up and have morning devotions, pass on the dessert, volunteer to help with the toddlers—only to have "Brother Donkey" rebel and insist on sleeping in, grabbing the largest dessert helping or declaring that he is much too worn-out after working all week to deal with toddlers.

Francis would sometimes have to throw Brother Donkey into the snow and slush if he wouldn't stop lusting after the cute milkmaid . . . which, upon consideration, is not such a terrible idea. (I wonder what the milkmaid thought when all of a sudden this young man coming down the road hurled himself headlong into a pile of mucky snow for no apparent reason? Must have been a hoot.)

I seem to recall that the apostle Paul was stuck with Brother Donkey as well. He claimed that he tried to "mortify" his donkey, which is where the monks probably got the idea that Brother Donkey would behave if you whacked away on him with whips.

But no, Brother Donkey can be very difficult to get with the program. Brother Donkey seems to think that his pleasures, agendas and wants are not to be denied. Brother Donkey scoffs at the notion of conversion, and to be controlled he must be bridled.

The Bible tells us that one of the events we can look forward to is the eventual conversion of Brother Donkey from a cranky, demanding and ultimately failing mechanism of flesh into some kind of really fun physical body (yes, the idea that we are raised incorruptible in some kind of physical way is clearly a Christian idea).

I like to ponder the possibilities of this kind of body. I presume it will be like the resurrected body of Jesus that, from the Gospel accounts, seemed to be designed of some kind of odd multidimensional stuff. Recall that He could walk into a closed and locked room, spooking the tar out of the already skittish disciples.

Sounds like fun!

He could hike with you for miles and, in some kind of cloaking device, not be recognized until He decided to be. Yet He could join in chowing down during a fish fry or be touched and handled as genuine by human mortals.

Very strange.

I wonder if the new model we trade in our tired carcass for will have the appearance of age or gender. I wonder if we will have skin color, straight or curly hair or perfectly aligned white teeth.

I wonder if our new body will be impervious to hot or cold, wet or dry or subject to gravity. I wonder if I will, like God, be outside of space and time so that I can travel at the speed of thought. Then I wonder if I will have any memories of life on earth, especially the pleasurable ones: an incredible sunset, the birth of a child, a moment of spiritual awakening, the love of another mortal. Or will hoping to recall even the best of these human pleasures be like asking if I will remember my car in the parking lot of Disneyland once I pass the turnstile into the Magic Kingdom?

The irony of being saddled with a dimension (my flesh) that remains at times very obstinate after the conversion of my heart and mind is an interesting aspect of the Christian faith.

Jesus recognized it after chewing out Peter and friends for snoring away during the very moments they should have been praying their guts out (see Matt. 26:40-41). But then He points out the incongruity between what they wanted to do and what they were able to get Brother Donkey to do by saying, "the spirit is willing, but the body is weak" (v. 41, *NIV*).

Paul griped about the same thing. His words show the frustration he had with Brother Donkey: "It happens so regularly that it's predictable. The moment I decide to do good, sin is there to trip me up. I truly delight in God's commands, but it's pretty obvious that not all of me join in that delight. Parts of me covertly rebel, and just when I least expect it, they take charge" (Rom. 7:21-23, *THE MESSAGE*).

Now, I bring up the obvious to point out something that is not so obvious.

What is true of our flesh is also true about a whole pile of other things inside of our supposedly converted little hearts. We are not converted in total, in spite of what we initially think has happened to us. We are converted in parts and pieces.

The old theologians came up with a term for this process and gave it a $10 name: *sanctification*. Sanctification really means being converted in pieces. The idea tells us that while we might make a significant and life-changing act of faith in Christ, that is merely the first step in a transformation project that has a total makeover as the end goal.

You see, when I became a believer, I honestly thought, *That's it! All I have to do now is to grow spiritually and enjoy the ride.* It never occurred to me that I would have any more converting to do since I was already "converted."

But the fact is, my pockets are loaded with currency of another world that I keep wanting to spend in God's kingdom. It has absolutely no value here, and it must be converted to be of any use at all.

I keep finding pieces of myself that are as stubborn as Brother Donkey.

And I am not alone. This, in spite of wishful thinking to the contrary, is the lot of every believer.

The fascinating thing is how God hammers away on some unconverted part of one guy while seemingly ignoring the same unconverted part in another person. (I have learned that God will get around to all the parts sooner or later; it's just that He has a different agenda with each of us.)

Some people have areas that are very difficult to convert. I know people who have been Christians for decades but still have an unconverted wallet. For some the sticking point is their tendency to explode in anger and say or do things that they regret deeply after they cool off. For others it is the silly things from their old way of thinking or living that they want to hang on to as a souvenir.

It is amazing what people will drag with them on the journey.

It is my understanding that the various trails used by sojourners who migrated across the Great Plains to the promised land in the West were littered with the remains of pianos, chests and furniture, which were bit by bit cast out of covered wagons. Apparently, those items initially packed as essentials were found to be less than helpful as the travelers made the arduous journey across Indian country, the steep mountain passes and muddy river bottoms.

Actually, it is amazing what I will drag with me on the journey.

My friend Craig is an avid backpacker. I don't mind a good hike if there is something worth finding at the end of the trip—like a treasure chest or a gold mine. But Craig assured me that a hike way above the tree line of the High Sierras would be worth it.

He described the beauty of crystal-clear lakes, pure water streams, brilliant star-studded skies and incredible views. He didn't mention that the lakes were too icy cold to swim in, that the menu was dehydrated food and that numbing temperatures and rock-laden ground would make sleeping miserable. But he did say we would have to carry all of our own stuff, so pack only the essentials.

Sensing an adventure, I signed up to go with him

While camping at the upper end of the tree line, trying to acclimate to the elevation before setting out on our hike, it occurred to me that we would be living off powdered Tang for a week and that I would sorely miss my daily fix of Dr. Pepper.

So I slipped a can of the nectar of the gods in my backpack and lugged those 12 fluid ounces all the way up to 12,000 feet.

By the time I got up to 12,000 feet, those 12 ounces felt like a couple of pounds. But I was determined to keep the soda for the very end of the trip to celebrate a return to civilization by slowly sipping the bubbly sugar on the last day.

What I didn't realize was that after cracking open the can my fellow hikers would look at me with longing and expectant stares, making it imperative that I share my private stash with them. All that extra effort for a thimbleful of pleasure!

I am afraid the backpack of my journey with Christ has been filled with all kinds of odds and ends of the world I supposedly left behind. But unlike my hiking trip, it turns out that I am not alone in dragging along unhelpful items; my fellow travelers are equally foolish and sometimes even surprised at what they find stashed away in their hearts.

I think I need to throw Brother Donkey into the snow and slush more often.

Now the Lord is the Spirit, and where the Spirit of the Lord is, there is freedom. And we, who with unveiled faces all reflect the Lord's glory, are being transformed into his likeness with ever-increasing glory, which comes from the Lord, who is the Spirit.

2 Corinthians 3:17-18, *NIV*

Be energetic in your life of salvation, reverent and sensitive before God. That energy is God's energy, an energy deep within you, God himself willing and working at what will give him the most pleasure.

Philippians 2:12-13, *THE MESSAGE*

Be imitators of God, therefore, as dearly loved children and live a life of love, just as Christ loved us and gave himself up for us as a fragrant offering and sacrifice to God.

Ephesians 5:1-2, *NIV*

Because of your partnership in the gospel from the first day until now, being confident of this, that he who began a good work in you will carry it on to completion until the day of Christ Jesus.

Philippians 1:5-6, *NIV*

19

ON THE HEELS
OF SUCCESS

When our eldest son, Mason, graduated from high school, we got him a new Martin acoustic guitar. We named it "Ludwig," and it was a very appropriate gift for a young man whose life's calling has been music. Ludwig serves him still.

A few years later, our second son, Justin, came up for graduation. We started to discuss with him what kind of gift he might want for this rite of passage. He had an unusual request: He wanted us to send him to the jungle—into the untouched reaches of the Amazon, to be specific.

Growing up, the boys had been fascinated with the wild and wooly jungle adventure stories told by my mentor, family friend and Indiana Jones clone, E. G. Von.

Every year Von headed into the deep, tangled jungles of South America, where he encouraged friends, missionary families and many of the offspring of his youth group who labored for Christ in the far reaches of civilization. And of course the missionaries would take this hearty and intrepid explorer with them over miles of uncharted jungle to rendezvous with naked Stone Age Indians who had not a clue about the modern world.

Often he would take along young men as traveling companions, and he said he would be happy to take Justin on one of his escapades.

Sending your graduate off to the most dangerous and isolated jungle in the world is not something you want to ponder for a long time. Horror stories of deadly snakes, poison-tipped spears and potentially hostile natives make you want to push for a trip to Cancun instead. But we set up the adventure and off he went.

After various pit stops in South America, and a long ride over the jungle in a very small plane, Von, Justin and a missionary found themselves at the head of a narrow trailhead in the Venezuelan jungle. Waiting for them were half a dozen barefoot, virtually naked Indians who were to serve as guides.

For an Indian, the jungle is the neighborhood. Each tree is a street sign; every small creek an intersection. Tall termite mounds are the corner 7-Eleven store, full of squishy, edible trail snacks. Trees that seem identical to those from the outside world have a look and personality to them as distinct as any suburban street.

The Indians have no problem reading the signs and navigating through the bush without fear of getting lost. Tiny, almost invisible trails are major sidewalks in their sight, and they know the difference between ones made by human feet and ones made by rooting boars.

To an outsider, the jungle is a terrifying and mysterious place. Death and disaster lurk everywhere. The foliage is dense and confusing. It is a place where even GPS technology is pointless.

The Amazon jungle has no cliffs, mountains or even large rocks; nothing to mark as a point of reference, only a vast canopy of trees. The only hope through the jungle are the Indian guides . . . and if they decide to up and leave you behind, you are pretty much toast.

The two men and the young high school grad who rolled out of the missionary plane that morning knew these facts and were determined to stay close to their guides during the trek to their village.

Shouldering their backpacks, they nodded to the natives and began to pace through the jungle.

The guides walked confidently along the faint trails that their visitors could not see. The sight of the Indians was the only trail marker the visiting men had, and Justin, taking one look at the dense forest around him, was determined not to lose track of them; so he started to close rank with the native who was walking well over a dozen feet in front of him.

The moment he did this, the Indian picked up speed, which in turn, caused Justin to pick up his gait as well. The Indian then moved faster and the visitors in turn hurried as well.

Before long the entourage was nearly running through the hot, steamy jungle.

Coming to a stream, the Indians and their guests stopped for a moment, exhausted and sweating.

"Why are we running?" asked the missionary, in between pants.

"We aren't the ones who want to run," puffed the Indian. "But you were coming so close behind us that we thought you were pushing us to go faster."

The missionary laughed and explained what had happened to the worn-out crew.

"They have a different sense of what it means to follow them in the jungle," he said. "We hike a few feet behind someone; but for these guys that is like stepping on their heels. In their culture, 'close' is half a dozen yards."

Justin groaned. In his desire not to lose his guides he had inadvertently caused a sprint through the hot jungle.

When our bug-bitten son related this anecdote to us upon his return, it occurred to me that it was a good example of how people end up being stampeded through life.

I could see a mirror reflecting myself in the story he told.

For example, as our children were growing up, there seemed to be some unspoken urgency to ensure that they were well rounded, multifaceted little human beings. This needed to be accomplished by hauling them from soccer practice to music lessons to foreign language class to martial arts and probably more if we, the parents, had not become utterly exhausted.

I don't know where the idea came from that kids would be better off having a hectic schedule than being left to play in the dirt. But the idea seems to be endemic.

And probably unnecessary; as a kid, I mostly played in the dirt, and I think I turned out fairly well rounded in spite of it.

So we had a family meeting where I insisted that we get away from the herd, let the kids get into what interested them and encourage them to play in the dirt more. My wife was cautious, but the kids thought the idea of dirt clods was way more appealing than Japanese School.

I think it was a wise move, and I suppose time will tell if all those kids on the stampeded track end up with lofty and academically brilliant careers while my kids stay close to the dirt by digging cesspools or something.

The urge to not be left in the jungle is played out in many ways.

Like a lot of guys (and maybe more than a few women), I feel the stampede to get the latest technological gadget or a speedier computer. There is this sense that the pack will run away from me, and without this new, faster collection of bells and whistles I may end up as a technological Neanderthal.

The economy of the world is built on the idea of staying on the heels of success, which of course ultimately leaves us breathless, broke and dissatisfied, since one can never seem to go fast enough to catch up.

Which of course is the trick.

From time to time people try to get off the squirrel wheel.

The Amish decided they were through with trying to keep up with all the new innovations of the industrial revolution and became a curiosity instead.

I am not quite sure it worked out the way they had originally planned.

Sometimes it feels as if I have found myself in a current that carries the whole of society along in the slow, gentle way that a riptide sucks you out to sea without your noticing it. We all want flat-screen TVs (just try selling your old tube model if you don't believe me); we all want to rear-end people with the "My child is an honor student at . . ." bumper sticker; we all end up buying an unlimited texting plan for our kid's cell phone.

Christians are no less subject to these stampedes than anyone else. In fact, we may be more so. Observe the trends that seem to animate large swaths of the Christian community and you will see people jump on the bandwagon of "what good Christians should do" without doing a whole lot of soul-searching, decision weighing or hard thinking.

I recall a time when many of my Christian friends started pulling their kids out of public school and sending them to private schools or homeschooling them.

Most everybody parroted the same thinking: "Public school is going to hell in a handbasket; it is time to abandon ship!"

"Wait a minute!" said I, who was too poor to afford private school and too busy and impatient to homeschool. "If all the Christians leave the public school system, how will we impact our culture and make changes?"

My objections fell on deaf ears, because the pace had been set and because according to the propaganda being promoted, the truly caring and truly good Christian parents would make sure their kids were insulated from rotten, pagan kids with bad language, and teachers who wanted to stuff evolution down the throats of unsuspecting students. Loving parents would at least properly prepare their brood to be academically equipped for a fine college, since the public school teachers are too busy writing referrals to do any quality teaching.

(I think I just lost a whole bunch of potential friends with this little roast of the pendulum swing toward isolating and insulating our kids. Sorry. My point is that this way of thinking about schooling is a *trend* that we believers often subscribe to without a whole lot of deep spiritual wrestling.)

I have come to understand that it is very difficult for me to live and think objectively. I have to work at it. And if I work hard at stepping back, rethinking, examining ideas, trends and cultural shifts in the light of God's Word (the unpleasant bits as well as the cherry-picked ones) and the prodding of the Holy Spirit, I find that I start living differently. Sometimes I end up living differently than many of my Christian friends.

I now try to save up for stuff I want, rather than reach for the instant gratification of a credit card, as I took the advice of Proverbs over the lure of the Visa card ads.

I turned off the cable. (My kids say, "*American Idol,* what is that?")

As a pastor, I insisted we close the church to activities on Halloween evening and urge the congregation to hand out full-size candy bars in their neighborhoods and send their kids out to trick or treat with their non-Christian friends. (We hand out toothbrushes *and* full-sized candy bars at our house, only because my wife is a dentist.)

I am trying to be earth friendly without being a sucker for people trying to make money out of those who are trying to be earth friendly. (I know it is a PC trend, but some trends actually make a little sense.)

I have friends who are Republican, Democrat and Libertarian . . . and I invite all of them to come to the same barbeque as long as they promise not to get into a fistfight.

I actually stop and think about what I am being prodded to chase after and pass on it . . . sometimes to the chagrin of some of my family members who are afraid that without this "necessary" thing, we will somehow become the new Amish.

And I don't have a flat screen TV.

Yet.

Don't fool yourself. Don't think that you can be wise merely by being up-to-date with the times. Be God's fool—that's the path to true wisdom. What the world calls smart, God calls stupid. It's written in Scripture, He exposes the chicanery of the chic. The Master sees through the smoke screens of the know-it-alls.

1 Corinthians 3:18-20, *THE MESSAGE*

If you decide for God, living a life of God-worship, it follows that you don't fuss about what's on the table at mealtimes or whether the clothes in your closet are in fashion. There is far more to your life than the food you put in your stomach, more to your outer appearance than the clothes you hang on your body. Look at the birds, free and unfettered, not tied down to a job description, careless in the care of God. And you count far more to him than birds. Has anyone by fussing in front of the mirror ever gotten taller by so much as an inch? All this time and money wasted on fashion—do you think it makes that much difference? Instead of looking at the fashions, walk out into the fields and look at the wildflowers. They never primp or shop, but have you ever seen color and design quite like it? The ten best-dressed men and women in the country look shabby alongside them. If God gives such attention to the appearance of wildflowers—most of which are never even seen—don't you think he'll attend to you, take pride in you, do his best for you? What I'm trying to do here is to get you to relax, to not be so preoccupied with getting, so you can respond to God's giving. People who don't know God and the way he works fuss over these things, but you know both God and how he works. Steep your life in God-reality, God-initiative, God-provisions. Don't worry about missing out. You'll find all your everyday human concerns will be met. Give your entire attention to what God is doing right now, and don't get worked up about what may or may not happen tomorrow. God will help you deal with whatever hard things come up when the time comes.

Matthew 6:25-34, *THE MESSAGE*

20

LOVE AND THE
VACUUM CLEANER

Sometimes it feels like I am in the cantina of a *Star Wars* movie. I am surrounded by odd creatures who speak a native tongue I can't understand. They process thoughts in an alien logic and have a lifestyle and habits that are so foreign as to be otherworldly.

So many strange people. I, of course, am normal.

Part of my own growth process as a believer has been to try to immerse myself in the odd world of these people and see if I can expand my understanding of what makes them tick.

I still can't relate to what motivates my friend Steve to turn his entire garage into a massive slot car track or understand why it thrills him to have slot cars from years ago still in their original packaging.

I don't understand the golf fetish that has overtaken some of my friends, making them spend big bucks to chase a white ball around in the hot sun. The best part about golf for me is when the eyes of the clown light up on the putt-putt course.

But the diversity of interests, passions and ways of thinking actually has helped educate me, has given me an appreciation for things I never appreciated and has stretched my ability to enfold all kinds of strange people into the category of brother and sister in Christ.

Arrogance about our own passions, interests or way of thinking shrinks us in our soul and makes us far more difficult to live with. Enlarging our ability to see things from another point of view or at least understand that there are other points of view really helps us to remove ourselves from the equation.

God, in His wisdom, seems to have the goal of removing ourselves from the equation as part of His overall plan. That, in my opinion, must be one of the reasons He factored in when He created men and women.

The ability to understand and love a creature so uniquely different from ourselves is not something that comes easily. We have to put focused energy into it, and we are not always successful . . . as my friend Annette found after her first year of marriage.

When Annette showed up for work she was obviously upset and agitated. I was her co-worker but it seemed like a good idea to become invisible until she cooled down. (This is typical male behavior when there is an agitated female ranting and raving in the vicinity.)

Around lunchtime Annette had sufficiently cooled to the point where she was ready to explain what had ignited her so dramatically; it was her stupid husband, Jim.

A few other women co-workers gathered around to hear her woeful tale and offer their sympathy. It was obvious that even though they had not heard the story, Jim was clearly guilty of whatever it was that happened. (I made a mental note to have women excluded from the jury if I was ever put on trial.)

It seems that Annette had high expectations for the couple's first anniversary. She was thrilled when Jim proudly carried a huge wrapped box into the room, kissed her and whispered, "Happy anniversary, honey, I love you," into her ear.

But when she tore into the gift, she found to her horror that the token of "love" her husband had presented her was a super-deluxe vacuum cleaner.

All the women in the group recoiled in shock when she explained what she had received from her husband.

"What did you do?" I asked.

"I just sat there and cried," she said.

"What did Jim do?" I continued.

"At first he thought I was happy . . . can you believe it? Then he wanted to know what was wrong."

"And you said . . . ?"

"I said nothing," declared Annette. "I just got mad that he was *so* dense that he couldn't figure it out!"

"Did that help?" I asked. "Did he understand why you reacted the way you did to the vacuum cleaner?"

Annette responded somewhat sheepishly, "Well, no. To be honest, we got in a huge fight and I ended up storming out of the house and going to the mall where I bought myself something nice for our anniversary."

The women around the table cooed in approval of Annette's response to the marital crisis.

Sensing there was more to the story, I prodded, "Why do you think it occurred to Jim to buy you a vacuum cleaner?"

Annette was silent for a moment and then said, "Well, a couple of weeks ago we were at the mall, and I remember seeing a fancy vacuum cleaner in the window of a shop and telling Jim that it would be nice to have something like that, because the vacuum I am using is on its last legs."

"Ah," I said. "So you actually indicated to your husband that the fancy vacuum cleaner was something you wanted!"

"Well, yes, but *NOT* for an anniversary present," Annette responded with flustered reaction.

"Look, I think you might need to see this from a guy's perspective," I said. "If you gave Jim a shop vacuum for an anniversary gift he would be deeply appreciative, because most guys like practical gifts. If you gave him a bundle of roses he would be perplexed and probably wonder why you were wasting money on him."

Annette nodded as I continued, "So I would imagine that Jim was probably trying to figure out what kind of gift you would like for your anniversary, and when you pointed to the vacuum cleaner he just thought like a normal guy and figured that you were hinting. And, I bet it was an expensive vacuum cleaner with all the bells and lights."

"Yeah," Annette sighed. "I *did* want a new vacuum cleaner, but just not for my anniversary."

"Well, I understand that because I have been married for a while, but you guys are on year one, so you've got some work in figuring out the man/woman thing still ahead of you.

"Look, Jim gave you that gift because he loves you and thought that it was what you wanted, because you *said* it was what you wanted. When you got upset, he felt frustrated, confused and unappreciated. What we have here is a classic failure in communication!"

The other women chimed in about how guys should know better anyhow, but I think Annette got the picture and understood that Jim, in spite of his clumsiness, really did love her. At least she went home that day in a different frame of mind; and after a good talk, both of them were laughing at how the whole situation took place.

I was so pleased with the results that I thought maybe I should start a side business in marriage counseling.

Now, I must admit, I understand Jim a lot more than I understand Annette. I like gifts that are functional, practical and not sentimental. I can't understand intellectually why women would want a dozen roses that blossom and die when they could have a Venus Flytrap that keeps on working for a living. Yet, trying to get my head around how women, and in particular my wife, think has been very helpful to my development as a Christian. It has made it so that life was not run by my realities, my rules and my sensibilities . . . unless I wanted to sleep with the dog.

I have a sense that many of the conflicts that we mortals find ourselves in are similar. Unspoken expectations, missed cues and misinterpreted signals are the root cause of conflict, not a lack of love or concern.

I am not taking anything away from the fallen nature of mankind or the fact that many of us have a nasty streak of selfishness, but I think that many times our conflicts come not so much from those elements but from misinterpretation or our inability to get the facts straight before we come to a conclusion.

At least I want to go there first before I write off the unbecoming behavior of a friend or a loved one to their being in cahoots with the devil.

I feel this way because it is mostly true about me. I don't get up in the morning plotting how to exasperate my wife, annoy my children and irritate the dog. For the most part, I am just trying to get the sleep out of my eyes and lose morning mouth. If I hog the bathroom or let something not so wonderful tumble out of my mouth, or if I neglect, ignore or give a slight, it is more likely the result of a still befuddled mind than evil intent.

I hope that my family will cut me some slack and offer some understanding. I hope they will know that I love them and care about them even if I can't recall their names if it is very early in the morning.

I want my wife to understand that I am thinking about her even if I bring home a nice new skillet as a Christmas present instead of some emotional gift. (Have you ever watched a guy try to go shopping for an emotional gift? It is like hunting for Sasquatch.)

And I promise I will try to understand and believe that she loves me and is thinking about me even if she insists that we watch *Pride and Prejudice* for the hundredth time despite the fact that there is a game on.

It may sound a bit Pollyanna-ish, but I want to apply this positive spin not just to my nuclear family but to my brothers and sisters in the church as well. I think that far too often we act as if we need to protect our church from the sin nature that resides in us all rather than trust that we live in a redemptive community where most people are actually getting better.

You end up with fewer locks, rules and committees if you see those you are doing Kingdom work with as saints instead of sinners.

I want to err on the side of love. I want to presume and hope for the best. I want to love people in spite of their quirks and oddities, and I want them to love me even if they somehow, in their own delusions, think I have quirks or am odd.

I know I might be disappointed from time to time, but in spite of that, it is a much happier way to live.

> *Love is patient, love is kind. It does not envy, it does not boast,*
> *it is not proud. It is not rude, it is not self-seeking, it is not easily*
> *angered, it keeps no record of wrongs. Love does not delight in evil*
> *but rejoices with the truth. It always protects, always trusts,*
> *always hopes, always perseveres.*

1 Corinthians 13:4-7, *NIV*

*So, chosen by God for this new life of love, dress in the wardrobe
God picked out for you: compassion, kindness, humility, quiet
strength, discipline. Be even-tempered, content with second place,
quick to forgive an offense. Forgive as quickly and completely as the
Master forgave you. And regardless of what else you put on, wear
love. It's your basic, all-purpose garment. Never be without it.*

Colossians 3:12-14, *THE MESSAGE*

21

THE HAIR SHIRT

When Germany's King Henry IV marched through northern Italy in the eleventh century, he appeared like any other wealthy member of royalty to the public who watched him ride into town with his entourage.

Clothed in thick, deliciously soft velvet robes trimmed with fur and laced with real gold thread and precious stones, the apparel alone would have made it apparent to peasants and townsmen alike that this man was worthy of admiration.

Little did those bowing and scraping the ground in homage know that the powerful German king was in secret misery. Through teeth-gritting smiles and happy hand waves he was scratching, itching and being rubbed raw at every jog of his great steed—for he was wearing a hair shirt.

He may have looked stylish and comfortable to everyone else, but he was not.

A hair shirt was a vest-like undershirt that was made up of the coarse skin and bristly hair of a goat or similar animal. The hair was turned toward the skin, and due to its stiffness caused the wearer a great deal of discomfort. The hair turned out not only to be prickly but it served as a wonderful hiding place for fleas, lice and other vermin.

Now, we modern minds often wonder at the strange antics of those medieval folks. What would possess a rich, powerful man to strap on this instrument of slow torture?

The wearer of a hair shirt put it on as punishment and penance for wrongdoing. (And King Henry had a huge laundry list of bad deeds.)

In the days before Christian psychoanalysts, hair shirts were quite the rage among the believing set. Saint Francis had one, as did Charlemagne and Saint Patrick. Thomas Becket was wearing one when he was murdered.

Literal hair shirts went out of fashion in the Christian community when the Reformation swept through. Those believers leading the reform movement dusted off a long neglected and ignored core idea of the Christian faith: *grace*.

Their rediscovered message was simple, powerful and unmatched to this day by any other "religious" system or theology.

Grace meant that the price had been paid for those wrongdoings. It brought freedom from the self-torture of guilt or the need to somehow pay for our moral and spiritual debts.

Grace was (and is) the polar opposite of karma. We get what we don't deserve, could never earn or attempt to pay for: absolute forgiveness for our sins, membership in the family of God, and life that beats death. It is the most thundering free gift that can be imagined.

But for many of us, the idea of grace is too simple.

We would rather find a hair shirt of some kind.

I have a hair shirt stowed away in the closet of my mind. Sometimes it begs me to put it on in order to prove that I am worthy of God's pardon and that I need to get out there and perform a deed or work harder to validate my Christianity and pay back grace. But over the years, as I have come to comprehend grace, I have gotten pretty good at keeping it boxed up and quiet.

I do have friends who seem to like to wear their hair shirt. Oh, on the outside they carry themselves as if they have it all together. They talk using Christian lingo and tote well-worn Bibles. But down there next to their skin they allow the guilt of long-forgiven sins to pinprick them and trouble them.

Some of them have a hair shirt that makes them work too hard for the church, as if this will relieve the itch. For others the hair shirt keeps them from ministry. They allow their hair shirt to act up in discomfort whenever they think about taking on responsibility of one kind or another. "If they ever knew the things you have done, they would never trust you," the shirt itches. And they believe the message of the hair shirt.

Some have Christian lives that are stiff and lifeless because their hair shirt demands that they live colorless and sterile in order to be worthy of forgiveness.

Some strap on the hair shirt and walk through the Christian life with the chafing reminder that they are not worthy to receive the gift without applying some kind of penalty to themselves.

Not only do we put on the hair shirt ourselves, but we also sometimes peddle the misery to others. From time to time I meet Christian people who want to make sure that someone who has failed spectacularly is mandated to wear a hair shirt.

Now, don't get me wrong, I believe in "just desserts." If you rob a bank and then come to faith in Christ, I think you should expect to go to jail and not be let off because God has forgiven you of your heist—not even if you return all the money and say you are sorry to all those you terrorized. People should not expect to be immune from the logical earthly consequences of our sins just because we have come to our senses and confessed them.

Grace operates on a completely different level.

One of my friends had a failing of a sexual nature—to be exact, a failing of a homosexual nature. He was horrified at himself; and those who had trusted him to be a moral example were horrified as well.

He couldn't take back the incident; the collapse of his world was instant and irrevocable.

Life was unbearable; overwhelming guilt and self-loathing consumed him.

Then came grace, mercy and forgiveness flooding from the cross, transversing time and this century, this culture, this horrid situation and this particular soul.

He was clean. He was free. His debt was erased, forgotten for eternity.

The self-loathing abated and he floated in the sweet water of God's grace.

But not all the Christians were happy about it. Oh, there was a universal applause for getting things right with God, but many wanted more. They wanted my friend to wear a hair shirt.

They wanted him to get up every morning, look at himself in the mirror and slip on the garment of torture and say, "I can't be trusted, I can't be lovable, I can't be normal, for I am a pervert."

And many Christians do just that. They slip on the hair shirt and say, "I am an adulteress," "I am a crook," "I am a liar," "I am lazy," "I am tainted," "I am addicted" or any other script designed for them by their failures.

In this way, the hair shirt makes a mockery of grace.

It is my understanding that the church of the first century often practiced a form of baptism that probably wouldn't fly in Kalamazoo.

Those who were about to go under the water were asked to strip off all of their clothes and be plunged into the water as naked as the day they were born.

There on the bank lay the garments of their old life, the ones that marked their rank and status, the ones everyone saw and the hidden ones, the hair shirt and all. In these early Christian communities, after the baptism, those garments were replaced with brand-new ones that were draped on the new convert, a symbol of being clothed anew in Christ.

Grace gives us new clothes to wear.

I tell my friends who feel the pressure to label themselves by the sin that once ruled their life to simply refer to themselves as "a sinner saved by grace." I tell them to lose the hair shirt.

Grace gives us the only garments we need to clothe ourselves in.

Now God has us where he wants us, with all the time
in this world and the next to shower grace and kindness upon
us in Christ Jesus. Saving is all his idea, and all his work.
All we do is trust him enough to let him do it. It's God's gift
from start to finish! We don't play the major role. If we did,
we'd probably go around bragging that we'd done the
whole thing! No, we neither make nor save ourselves.
God does both the making and saving.

Ephesians 2:7-10, *THE MESSAGE*

Because of his grace he declared us righteous and gave us
confidence that we will inherit eternal life.

Titus 3:7, *NLT*

22

A USELESS TALENT

I have a useless talent.

It is a gift really, a skill I never had to develop, that has been mine since I was a young boy.

I can instantly spot Indian pottery on the ground.

When I was a kid my parents would often take us camping in the desert areas that lay at the backside of substantial California mountains. We would stay in state parks, many of which were built in areas that once had been inhabited by Native Americans.

These now absent indigenous folk had a *lot* of clay pots.

For reasons I have never understood they seemed to break a lot of them, too, and the shards from these broken containers found their way across the desert floor, mixing in with sand and other rocks.

I could immediately detect the subtle difference in texture that showed a remnant to be a piece of Indian pottery instead of a small rock. During our stays in the desert, I would fill my pockets with the small brown chunks of pottery. Sometimes I would find an orphaned piece that had once formed part of a bowl lip or handle. These were starring pieces in my collection.

By the time I was in fifth grade, I could "track" the ancient Indian settlers by following the shards of their pottery. By discovering increasingly richer pottery-picking fields, I knew I was approaching a place that had once been an Indian settlement or hangout of some kind.

No one was particularly impressed with my useless talent.

"Why do you keep picking up rocks from the ground?" my sister would ask.

"They are not rocks; they are pieces of Indian pottery," I would reply.

"Who cares? They are just a little tiny piece, not a whole pot or anything of value!" she would say.

And she was right.

But I had a gift, and it was hard not to walk around on that desert floor without stooping down to snag another pottery shard to place in my bulging pockets.

My mother gave me an empty mayonnaise jar to put the shards in. Apparently pottery pieces made a racket if they found their way into the dryer.

Several mayonnaise jars later, we took another trip to the desert. I wanted to go hunting for tarantulas or see if we could scare up a rattlesnake; these endeavors and adventures seemed more akin to what a *real boy* ought to be doing, but I ended up tracking pottery shards again.

But this time it was different.

My pottery-finding Geiger counter was in overdrive.

The shards led me out of the desert floor and into a small valley cut out of severe rocks. The shards were everywhere. My brother, who had tagged along, couldn't see a one of them but watched in awe as I whirled around, scooping them up as fast as I could.

"Here's one, here's another and another," I squealed in excitement.

The trail let to a jumbled rock outcropping that seemed to have once contained some kind of old pit.

And there I saw it, deep under the pile of rocks: a whole Native Indian pot.

It was cracked, and the neck was ajar from the body of the pot, but it was not a shard, it was the whole thing—the holy grail of Indian pottery-shard pickers.

I was ready to start excavation then and there, but an adult hiker stumbled upon us and convinced us to tell the park ranger, which being dutiful children we did.

The next thing I knew the Indian pot was on its way to an archaeologist and probably to a museum somewhere.

The ranger thanked me for reporting the find. He thought I had merely stumbled upon it. He didn't know about my gift, and I never told him.

But for some reason the gift did not seem so useless anymore. It had been used to make a contribution to science or history. Someone was no doubt categorizing my discovery and tenderly piecing it back together as I filled another mayonnaise jar. If it had not been for my useless talent, the handiwork of some ancient people would have remained hidden and unappreciated.

Seemingly useless talents abound.

I think God gives them to us, and most of the time without explanation or user instructions.

Sometimes those gifts are quite odd. The ability to sniff out a phony; the ability to sense when someone is hurting; a natural way with words; an instinctive grace with color and balance; ease with numbers, with abstract ideas, with animals; or an innate sense of rhythm; all are gifts that may appear to be nothing more than oddities. (Especially the ability to find pottery on the desert floor.)

We Christians often celebrate the spiritual gifts that are spelled out in the letters of Paul but give scant attention to these unique and peculiar little talents so generously scattered to all humankind. Would these odd-shaped gems be any less spiritual in nature just because their purpose is so narrow or eccentric?

Perhaps God inserts these sometimes strange talents into people in order to give some kind of vivid color to humanity. After all, if we all were cookie cutter replicates of each other the world would be pretty boring.

Perhaps God passes around seemingly useless talents because they are not entirely useless. After all, one never knows when one might need the service of a pottery spotter, or a gift that a friend of mine has that allows him to *instantly* know how many *letters* are in any word without even seeing it; spaghetti—"nine." (Don't ask me exactly what you can do with a gift like that, maybe win on a game show or something.)

Regardless, I think it is important for us to embrace our oddities, strange abilities and natural talents not as useless gifts but as something unique that God may somehow, even for a brief moment, want to use.

I once worked with a woman who had a natural sense of how the English language should flow. She could spot a misspelled word or error in grammar in an instant. She could take even the clunkiest sentence and rearrange it to give it flow and beauty. She was actually the "ghost" behind the authors of some of the "greatest hits" of modern Christian publishing (although she never received credit for her ghostwriting). Strangely enough, in spite of her immense talent with words, she had a very difficult time coming up with an original idea of her own. She was a word person, not an idea person; but she could sure spot a good idea and make it sing. Her ability was to take random, poorly written ideas scrawled on yellow pads and turn them into useful books.

People who bought, enjoyed and recommended those popular books never knew that there was someone with a strange and unique gift hidden in the words they were reading.

In literature, this is nothing new.

Would the letter Peter wrote to the scattered believers have had the beautiful Greek tone without the natural translation talent of the unknown "amanuensis" or scribe who almost all scholars believe took the rough Galilean's words and smoothed them into words of a professional orator? Even the apostle Paul used one of these guys—Tertius, who even got credit for his skill (see Rom. 16:22).

I enjoy the fact that many times it takes awhile to discover the really cool abilities some people have concealed inside of them.

I have a friend who is an incredible musician and poet. His lyrics are deep, thoughtful, profound, and they show insight that marvels those who hear his music. The funny thing is that if you hung around with him you would never know it. His less than polished social skills and hesitant conversation never give a hint to the gift hidden within.

There is something wonderful in seeing the spectrum of God-given talents in action. The culture (and often the church) celebrates only a tiny slice of those gifts. But where would we be without the person who has an uncanny skill of organization, or the comic who can bring us to tears laughing at his hilarious gift of perfect mimicry, or the rare duck who somehow has the ability to love and communicate to middle-schoolers?

Are these gifts "spiritual gifts"?

I don't know. Maybe.

I am not sure why God would give someone a nose for finding Indian pottery. It certainly is not a gift the world is clamoring to celebrate.

But all these tiny, quirky gifts seem to be the very things that give dimension, possibility, exploration, imagination and a beautiful tint to those created in God's image.

> *Every desirable and beneficial gift comes out of heaven. The gifts are rivers of light cascading down from the Father of Light.*
>
> James 1:17, *THE MESSAGE*

> *Observe people who are good at their work—skilled workers are always in demand and admired; they don't take a back seat to anyone.*
>
> Proverbs 22:29, *THE MESSAGE*

> *I know that there is nothing better for men than to be happy and do good while they live. That everyone may eat and drink, and find satisfaction in all his toil—this is the gift of God.*
>
> Ecclesiastes 3:12-13, *NIV*

> *Do you see a man skilled in his work? He will serve before kings; he will not serve before obscure men.*
>
> Proverbs 22:29, *NIV*

23

THE STATUE

I often get a bad feeling about the spiritual prospects of some people.

If I were a betting man, I would place my money on the dynamic spiritual growth and longevity of some individuals (especially those who are bright, warm, achiever types) and wouldn't put a dime on the sustainability of others.

And if I were putting down a wager, I would often be broke.

You see, I am consistently surprised in which souls the Word takes root and blossoms and which souls end up merely checking out the Jesus thing or passing through a "religious stage" before moving on to supposedly greener fields, in spite of how much love and care are shown to them by mentor types.

And the ones who hang in there and the ones who don't are not always who you think they would be.

As a youth pastor, I had kids from sterling Christian families (some of them missionaries) end up as career criminals, and kids who came from families that could be used to define the word "dysfunctional" end up being well-rounded, dynamic believers.

The Bible tells us that the ways of the Lord are mysterious. They are also very bizarre and counterintuitive.

Jenny was one kid for whom I didn't have a lot of hope outside of a miracle. Friendly and animated, her background was the stuff of nightmares. Mom had a good-sized drug habit and decided to make her middle-school daughter a party pal.

By the time she stumbled into eighth grade, Jenny had the life experiences that would shock a pulp fiction writer.

Jenny showed up at our youth meetings, invited by a friend.

I was never sure how much was sinking in, and kids like this usually tell their youth worker what they think he or she wants to hear. I was hopeful that some God-stuff was getting through, but I also would not have been shocked if she drifted away.

Because so many of these kids were from deeply pagan cultures, I usually kept the Bible study portion of the meeting centered around the adventures of Jesus and His teaching. I taught about things that I hoped the kids would relate to or remember: the prodigal son, Zacchaeus the tax collector, the woman who washed the feet of Jesus with tears.

The kids seemed to listen and enjoy these stories, but you never quite knew what was sinking into the soul.

Jenny would show up to hear these meetings and then go out and party with her friends. It was a weird mix of messages and influences. People who inhabit that world usually end up tilting in the direction of sin. It is, after all, their natural language and environment.

But God is not to be underestimated, even in the life of a totally messed-up eighth-grade girl.

Late one night, Jenny was roaming around our one-horse town with a couple of her party friends. They were high as kites and bored silly. It was well after midnight and nothing was open.

"Let's go to church," suggested one of them, pointing to the Catholic church, which had an open 24/7 policy.

The idea seemed so outrageous, offbeat and goofy that Jenny and the other drugged-out girls thought it sounded like fun. Besides, it had started to drizzle, and going inside the building would get them out of the rain.

No priest was awake as the girls, suppressing giggles, slipped through the front door. One of them splashed the other with holy water, and they wandered around the building, finally plopping down on a back pew.

For a while the statuary, the stained glass and the crucified Jesus, high behind the altar, gave these unchurched girls a strange visual feast.

But boredom once again set in and the girls became restless.

"Let's get outta here," one said.

"Yeah, I'm over it," said another as she stood to her feet.

But Jenny didn't move.

Something was stirring inside of her. Thoughts deeper, harder, condemning and yet comforting crashed against the drugs in her system and melted them away.

God was calling her, inviting her to something she had never known: love, acceptance, forgiveness.

"I want to stay for a while," she said to her friends.

"Suit yourself," one said, and they disappeared into the darkness.

Jenny bowed her head and recalled the stories she had heard about Jesus. She knew He was calling to her, but He was up there, out of reach, high above the wall.

She pulled herself out of the pew and stepped out into the black, wet night.

Then she saw Him; He stood on a brick pedestal in the center of a small garden, white alabaster arms outstretched: Jesus.

She approached the statue and then fell to its feet, wrapping her arms around the hard carved legs.

And she began to weep.

Jenny wept for the innocence she had lost, for the craziness that passed as normal to her, for the things she had done. Like the Bible story she had heard about the woman who washed Jesus' feet with her tears, Jenny wept on the feet of Jesus and then dried the tears that pooled on those stone feet with her hair.

I believe that in those quiet moments, those feet of alabaster actually became the feet of Jesus. Not in a miraculous sense, but in a way more real and genuine than actually coursing with flesh and blood.

That took place nearly 20 years ago.

The white statue of Jesus still stands on his brick pedestal with arms outstretched.

And that night, Jenny made it.

She stepped into faith and never let go.

I saw her yesterday—a wife, a mother. She was smiling and laughing, happily directing young teenage girls toward the meeting room at a camp her youth pastor husband was running.

I didn't tell her that I would have bet against her making it spiritually.

My bets don't make any difference anyhow.

There is something at play here that I can't fathom. It is a mystery, like God Himself.

> God's wisdom is something mysterious that goes deep into the
> interior of his purposes. You don't find it lying around on
> the surface. It's not the latest message, but more like the oldest—
> what God determined as the way to bring out his best in us, long
> before we ever arrived on the scene. The experts of our day
> haven't a clue about what this eternal plan is. If they had, they
> wouldn't have killed the Master of the God-designed life on a
> cross. That's why we have this Scripture text: No one's ever seen
> or heard anything like this, never so much as imagined anything
> quite like it—what God has arranged for those who love him.
> But you've seen and heard it because God by his Spirit has
> brought it all out into the open before you.
>
> 1 Corinthians 2:7-10, *THE MESSAGE*

24

THE CHINA CUPBOARD

Somebody once told me that you can know what a person *really* values by looking at his or her checkbook entries or credit card summaries.

Jesus said as much when He slyly reminded His baffled followers that "where your treasure is, there your heart will be also" (Matt. 6:21, *NIV*).

The "heart" is the prime conspirator in the actions, choices and values of human beings. The Bible would define the "heart" as the seat of our emotions.

Most of us try to tell ourselves that we run the affairs of our lives unaffected by the tangle of any emotional (heart) strings. Sure, we have emotions, but we also have the good sense not to let them get in the way of our behavior.

But that is not *really* true. We only have to pause and look at our own actions to disprove the notion that we are not emotionally compromised.

Some of us buy food we are not hungry for simply to *feel good*.

Some may pick a vehicle to purchase, not for raw economic reasons or practicality but because it carries an *emotional message* of power, prestige or style.

We most often choose friends, church communities and activities because they make us *feel comfortable*, and not because we particularly have weighed out our choices in cool Mr. Spock-like logic.

Our feelings, moods and emotions are whirled into *every* decision we make, even if we present ourselves as emotionally detached, rational machines.

And our emotions can be crazy as a loon.

It has been hard for me to come to grips with this in my own life.

I come from emotionally cool Germanic stock. I have a distinctly set personal space that you are not allowed to come into without invitation, thank you.

I don't care much for hugs, especially ones that last more than a micro-second. I don't care to receive them and I am not likely to hand them out either. Unless you are family, please don't come to me *expecting* a hug. If you get even the semblance of one it is only because I let down my guard. (Some of you huggers really don't like me anymore, do you?)

I keep a tight rein on my emotions and often hold in quiet contempt those who, as a lifestyle, ride the emotional pendulum.

If I won the lottery or a sweepstake contest, I would probably not believe it (I am a skeptic by nature); and then if proven to be true, I would no doubt just smile gently and say, "That's cool." (In contrast to some of my friends who would be running up and down the street in their underwear screaming for joy.)

I admire Sherlock Holmes's detached and penetrating powers of observation but am aghast that his creator actually believed in woodland fairies. (What a sucker!)

You get the picture.

People like me (and there are a lot of us) don't think there is an ounce of emotion mixed in with our life decisions, and it is hard for us to fathom people who seem to make strange and illogical choices based on some liquid, inequitable set of thoughts or feelings.

Yet I think sometimes we logic-and-reason types miss out on having the chance to peer through the window of a person's soul because we try to cram everything into the *makes sense* or *doesn't make sense* categories.

For the many years I lived in California, I was within short driving distance of Mexico. During my high school years, I would often take the 20-minute drive to the border in order to surf uncrowded beaches and help out with various ministries that worked among the vast but well-hidden people who lived in conditions of foul poverty. I could never get over the irony that whole families lived in horrid, floorless shacks within a few miles from the glitter and wealth of America.

With an overwhelming amount of needy hands to fill, over the years I settled on being committed to serving a particular group of kids who lived in a beat-up orphanage run by an old Mexican couple.

The man was called "Papa Torres." He was very old but had an adventurous past. The old guy had actually ridden with Pancho Villa; but I could never get him to talk about it.

The old lady was called, appropriately, "Mama Torres."

She was squat, toothless, dark, with a chewed-up complexion that betrayed years of hard work under a severe sun. She dressed layered in hand-me-downs and wore the classic shawl typical of the peasant class.

The place they ran was a hand-to-mouth operation. They had no mission or denominational affiliation, and the work they did came from the outcome of this kind woman and her husband who kept taking in kids whose parents had abandoned them until they accidentally had an "orphanage" going.

Like many similar institutions in Mexico, few of the kids were truly orphaned; most were the offspring of prostitutes, trysts or teenage mothers.

Inspired by the example of the nineteenth-century man of faith George Müller, the Torres family depended upon prayer to bring in the food and clothing they needed to provide for the kids.

They survived, but barely.

The kids usually slept two to a bunk, wore ratty clothes, had bad teeth and frequently suffered from the vermin that cohabit with this kind of poverty.

The strong smell of urine in some of the rooms—the result of bedwetters and no mattress covers—actually made my eyes water.

The toilet and shower facilities . . . well, let me put it this way, it made all of us want to hold back the call of nature until crossing the border.

We weren't the only ones who tried to sustain the Torres Orphanage (the official name was "House of Light"). Many other groups and individuals did what they could to help.

I visited regularly enough that the kids would run into the street chanting my name when they saw my surfboard-stacked vehicle turn off the highway (which, by the way, made me feel terrific).

One day, after distributing gifts of small toys and unloading food, Mama Torres grabbed me by the arm and asked me to follow her. Her English was nonexistent and my Spanish was dicey at best. It seemed like something urgent was up, so I called for someone to help translate.

We wound our way past the dingy dining room made of frigid, unpainted concrete block, past the kitchen where sanitation was a happy accident and into a small back room. There, amid sacks of rice and boxes of canned goods stood a brand-new china cupboard.

Mama Torres beamed at me happily and gestured toward the sparkling piece of furniture.

She was proud. Proud like the neighbor who pulls into the driveway with a new car. Proud and in awe, like when you lift a shiny new guitar out of the case for the first time or first plug in that new 50-inch high-def television.

I didn't understand and was confused. Why did she have a china cupboard? Mama Torres didn't own china. Heck, she didn't own two dishes that matched!

The old lady rattled off something in Spanish.

My translator nodded and then explained to me.

"Somebody gave Mama Torres some cash," she said. "They told her she had to spend it on herself, not on the children, not on food, but on herself. So this is what she bought. She said she had always wanted one."

The incongruity of the purchase for her environment couldn't have been more pronounced. I didn't quite know what to say, but seeing her beaming eyes looking up at me, I stroked the grain of the wood and said, *Muy bonita*—very beautiful.

The china cabinet had only one dish in it. It would never host another.

On the drive home, the logical part of me had a field day.

"What a nutty thing to buy!" I said to those traveling with me. "If I were her, I would have bought some dentures or something useful."

I have to admit, the mystery of why Mama Torres would buy a china cupboard for dishes she would never have bugged me for days. It seemed so odd, so unnecessary, so . . . pointless.

A cruel kind of judgment wanted to reign in my thoughts.

But then God began to whisper. "Try, try," He seemed to say to me. "Try to see the china cupboard from the perspective of Mama Torres."

Actually, there was no way my well-heeled, masculine, Yankee mind would ever be able to make logical sense of Mama Torres's china cupboard. Her purchase was *entirely* emotional, a heart thing, a dream thing, an action that came from some place I could never feel or even visit.

It came from deep and relentless poverty. It came from giving up the normalcy of home and family for a huge ministry of caring for others. It came from seeing the nicely dressed foreigners in new-model cars drop off their leftovers week after week. It came from never having two pesos extra to spend on herself.

To be frank, I still do not understand how people make these kinds of decisions. But I am okay with not understanding. I know there is an emotional element, irrational, incomprehensible and sometimes crazy that weaves itself into every choice we make.

It is the job of our mind to make sure that our heart doesn't make all the decisions (it is very prone to wickedness, you know); and it is the job of our heart to find a safe outlet to do something a little crazy once in a while.

It is what keeps us human.

But Mama Torres's china cupboard also was a good reminder to me that I need to be cautious about rushing to judgment about others. Mama Torres's crazy, illogical and pointless purchase made sense to her heart.

I am not suggesting that the whim to buy the big Harley Davidson or run naked through the forest ought to be followed. Most of our whims, urges and desires are better off going unanswered or should be checkmated by our trusty friend reason.

But every once in a while we need to let our heart run loose, too, without letting loose entirely of the reins of constraint. We may need to dance, to dress up silly, to plunge into a pool fully clothed or buy ourselves a train set for the garage. On some occasions it *might* be good for us to give in to the urge to buy an extra-large Butterfinger, to go out and pan for gold, to roll on the floor laughing at stupid jokes, to paint the wall chartreuse . . . or bring home something we don't have any use for.

It may just make us a bit more unpredictable, a tiny sliver more fun and perhaps a little more of a colorful Christian. And we will certainly confuse our rationally minded friends.

The poor will eat and be satisfied; they who seek the LORD will praise him—may your hearts live forever!

Psalm 22:26, *NIV*

The good man brings good things out of the good stored up in his heart, and the evil man brings evil things out of the evil stored up in his heart. For out of the overflow of his heart his mouth speaks.

Luke 6:45, *NIV*

As water reflects a face, so a man's heart reflects the man.

Proverbs 27:19, *NIV*

Don't pick on people, jump on their failures, criticize their faults—unless, of course, you want the same treatment. That critical spirit has a way of boomeranging.

Matthew 7:1-2, *THE MESSAGE*

25

ON HERMITS, SPECIAL DISHES AND HOLINESS

My mom had special dishes. I can still recall the brown-and-yellow color pattern that laced over the tableware. The funny thing is that decades later, I can still picture the plates and saucers in my mind, even though I *rarely* got to eat off of them. Those colorful ceramics were the VIP dishes, stored high above the easy grasp of any kid's greasy fingers.

We did use dishes in our house, more common everyday dishes, but I can't recall what they looked like or even their color. They were nicked, dinged and expendable. In fact, I think they were a mixed lot, orphans and refugees of different color and style whose siblings had been cracked or lost.

I think I remember the look of the special dishes because they were considered so hallowed that it had to be some very, very important guest or some incredibly high and holy occasion for them to see the light of day.

Those super-special events that would call for the super-special dishes were extremely rare and based on a criterion that was known only to my mother. I know that it did not include any milestones of "kiddom" such as birthdays, graduations, losing a tooth, leaving for college, and so on.

When someone first explained to me the idea of "holiness," the image of my mother's brightly colored dishes popped right into my head.

Holiness means being so special and so set apart that you are virtually useless in everyday life.

If you recoil at that definition, consider that while it may not be correct theologically, many times that is the very message we give when we call something "holy."

Christian people for centuries have defined holiness by creating criteria for holy living that often serves to make believers who subscribe to it nearly ineffectual in the everyday life they share with the unwashed masses.

Holiness standards were invisibly lacquered onto mere buildings through a mother's instruction to her children not to run, play, have fun or speak above a whisper because they were now in "God's House."

They were affirmed by making sure that the biggest room in "God's House" was both the least used and the most expensively adorned . . . because it was set apart, holy, to be used for one purpose only; thereby rendering it worthless for everyday goings-on.

Holiness was applied not just to buildings but also to how Christians presented themselves to the world.

The Puritans considered themselves "separatists" (think holy) to the point that they wouldn't allow their followers to dress in any joyous colors—drab brown and black obviously being God's preferred color scheme. (Never mind the vivid palette He used to paint creation.) They became so odd that they lost much of their effectiveness and became, in their home country, a target of persecution by their brightly dressed neighbors.

While growing up, I would meet Christian kids who couldn't relate to our gang when we talked about movies (and I am talking about Disney movies here) because someone decided that going to the movies was sure to make a holy kid unholy. The depth of their Christianity and their holiness was defined by what they didn't do.

We simply thought they were part of some weird cult like the kids who couldn't have a birthday party or get a Christmas present.

If you were to ask the religious leaders who shadowed Jesus around the Judean neighborhoods, they would have said that He had a holiness problem.

He went to parties that were populated with less-than-desirable types of people . . . and He seemed to enjoy Himself.

He struck up conversations with loose women; He palled around with crooks and traitors; He preferred the company of rough laborers to the religiously refined; He set up an instant winery; He hit people with whips.

Yet, He was 100 percent holy.

He was in the world, embedded deeply, experiencing in taste, smell, sight and emotion all that His creation experienced, yet He was set apart, holy, not of the world.

I find myself wanting to distance myself from those who define their holiness by all the stuff they don't do. I prefer the earthy holiness of someone like Martin Luther who, wiping the beer foam from his lips and squeezing his plump fraulein, would say some nasty things about the civil rights of peasants or Jews, pronounce on the worthlessness of the book of James and then turn around and say or do something of incredible spiritual depth.

Holiness is usually not found in those who are casting themselves in that role but more often in those who are so aware of their own unholiness and imperfection that all they can do is hope that there is room enough in grace for them. They are dinged, chipped and mismatched, but available as carriers of a message of mercy for the common man.

I ventured upon a parable by Tolstoy (who is another poster child for stumbling blindly and wildly after Jesus). I love it so much that I took the liberty of re-crafting it a bit and share it whenever I get a chance. It goes like this:

Once upon a time, many, many years ago, there was a bishop who had been quite successful in building a large flock. People loved his eloquent and witty teaching. They admired his depth of knowledge and the beautiful way he taught the Word of God.

Eventually, the success of this bishop attracted the attention of the pope, who invited him to sail to Rome to be honored.

The bishop and his followers were euphoric about this glorious tribute, and the bishop set sail with great fanfare and the blessings of his people.

The winds were with the ship, and a few days into the voyage, as the bishop leaned against the railing, he noticed a very small island coming into view.

"What is that island?" he asked the captain.

"I have never been there," replied the captain, "but I hear from fishermen who ply these waters that it is the home of three hermits."

The bishop was intrigued.

Three men so devoted to God that they would spend their lives on a small island such as this might be interesting to visit and, no doubt, they would be honored to have a personage such as myself visit them, he thought.

"Captain, would we have time for a short stop?" the bishop asked.

The captain furrowed his brow and said, "I might venture to say to your Grace that the old men are not worth your pains. I have heard that they are foolish old fellows who understand nothing and never speak a word, any more than the fish in the sea."

"I wish to go anyhow," said the bishop, and then added, "and if needs be, I will pay you extra for your trouble."

Since the winds had been so favorable that this stop would not interrupt their schedule, and since the bishop insisted, the captain gave the order for the rowboat to be readied.

Sliding into the tiny bay of the small island, the bishop could see the three old, ragged, thin men waiting anxiously for them on the sand.

The oarsmen drove the boat to the beach and helped the bishop off.

The old men immediately bowed to him, and he gave them his benediction, at which they bowed still lower. Then the bishop began to speak to them.

"I have heard," he said, "that you godly men live here saving your own souls, and praying to our Lord Christ for your fellow men. I, an unworthy servant of Christ, am called, by God's mercy, to keep and teach His flock. I wished to see you, servants of God, and to do what I can to teach you also."

The old men looked at each other and smiled but remained silent.

"Tell me," said the bishop, "what do you do to serve God?"

"We do not know very well how to serve God," replied the one who seemed to be oldest.

The Bishop was puzzled by his answer but then said, "Well, how do you pray?"

"We pray in this way," replied the hermit. "Three are You, three are we; have mercy upon us!"

The Bishop smiled.

"Well, you have evidently heard something of the Trinity," he said. And he began a lengthy explanation of the triune nature of God.

The old men stared at him blankly.

Sensing that he was not getting through to them, the Bishop readjusted his fine robes and decided to take another tack.

"At least I can teach you to pray. Do you know the Lord's prayer?"

The old men shook their heads, so the bishop began to instruct them.

The hermits repeated in fits and starts, "Our Father, who is in heaven, holy is your name."

As the lesson continued, they forgot words and whole sentences, yet the Bishop did not let off until the three old hermits had stumbled haltingly through the prayer.

It was getting dark, and the moon was appearing over the water as the Bishop dusted himself off and started back to the vessel.

On the beach, the old men bowed to the ground before him. He raised them and blessed each of them, telling them to pray as he had taught them. Then he got into the boat and returned to the ship.

"How did it go?" inquired the captain as the bishop boarded the ship.

"You are right, they are barely idiots," said the bishop, who then added, "Although I am glad I could take the time to teach them something."

The bishop was looking at the first stars to drift through the dusk when he heard a boatman make a startled cry from the stern of the ship.

The bishop turned and stared.

In the gray haze he could just barely make out three blobs of white upon the dark sea; it was the hermits. And as they came into focus it was clear that they were walking upon the water.

The bishop watched with mouth agape as they climbed up the rope onto the ship.

The three old men spotted the bishop and quickly bowed at his feet.

"We have forgotten your teaching, servant of God. As long as we kept repeating it, we remembered; but when we stopped saying it for a time, a word dropped out, and now it has all gone to pieces. We can remember nothing of it. Teach us again."

The bishop crossed himself. "Your own prayer will reach the Lord, men of God. It is not for me to teach you. Pray for us sinners."

The bishop went to his knees and bowed low before the old men; and they turned and went back across the sea. And a light shone until daybreak on the spot where they were lost to sight.

> *May God himself, the God who makes everything holy and whole, make you holy and whole, put you together—spirit, soul, and body—and keep you fit for the coming of our Master, Jesus Christ. The One who called you is completely dependable. If he said it, he'll do it!*

1 Thessalonians 5:23, *THE MESSAGE*

> *I can anticipate the response that is coming: "I know that all God's commands are spiritual, but I'm not. Isn't this also your experience?" Yes. I'm full of myself—after all, I've spent a long time in sin's prison. What I don't understand about myself is that I decide one way, but then I act another, doing things I absolutely despise. So if I can't be trusted to figure out what is best for myself and then do it, it becomes obvious that God's command is necessary. But I need something more! For if I know the law but still can't keep it, and if the power of sin within me keeps sabotaging my best intentions, I obviously need help! I realize that I don't have what it takes. I can will it, but I can't do it. I decide to do good, but I don't really do it; I decide not to do bad, but then I do it anyway. My decisions, such as they are, don't result in actions. Something has gone wrong deep within me and gets the better of me every time. It happens so regularly*

that it's predictable. The moment I decide to do good, sin is there to trip me up. I truly delight in God's commands, but it's pretty obvious that not all of me joins in that delight. Parts of me covertly rebel, and just when I least expect it, they take charge. I've tried everything and nothing helps. I'm at the end of my rope. Is there no one who can do anything for me? Isn't that the real question? The answer, thank God, is that Jesus Christ can and does. He acted to set things right in this life of contradictions where I want to serve God with all my heart and mind, but am pulled by the influence of sin to do something totally different.

Romans 7:14-25, *THE MESSAGE*

26

FROM THE ROOFTOPS

I came to realize much later in life that my mom, who I had always seen as staid and cautious, was really quite an adventurous woman.

As a very young woman, she escaped her South Dakota farm community by joining the U.S. Navy during World War II. After a tour of duty that took her from one end of the nation to the other, she bravely settled on the West coast, thousands of miles from any relative.

She couldn't swim a stroke, but that didn't stop her from grabbing an inflatable rubber mattress and wading out into the ocean as far as she could touch and riding the waves while laughing giddily all the way to the sand. I owe her for my happy addiction to the ocean.

She loved to explore both our nation and other places around the world, and when she had raised her brood, she would gallivant off here and there with retired friends who were also busy spending their children's inheritance.

But my mom had a secret that none of her friends knew about.

It came out on a thickly overcast fall day in Europe. My mother was on a whirlwind "if it's Tuesday this must be Belgium" kind of tour. She and her friends rode the luxurious touring bus across the Belgium border, passed the concrete dragon teeth—moldy remains from the war she had served in—and into Germany.

New tour guides came aboard, a new driver and front man to educate and entertain this group of American retirees.

The front man spoke English well, with only a hint of a German accent, and he treated his guests with jovial humor as they wove their way past medieval castles, thick forests and small Hansel and Gretel towns.

Each evening the group would bed down at a small hotel or inn, and after a hearty breakfast, they would continue exploring Germany through a bus window.

One morning, my mother took a seat at the front of the bus. The driver and guide began to talk and laugh in German. They had been with these elderly Americans for several days now, and they were having a bit of fun at their expense, talking derisively about many of them, all in the German language, of course.

The men laughed and exchanged jests as they headed down the country lane. Finally, when there was a break in their lampoon session, my mother spoke.

To the surprise of her friends, and especially to the bus driver and the guide, she spoke in perfect German, "You really should be more careful when you make fun of people. Some of us can understand everything you are saying."

The driver nearly crashed the bus.

The friends of my mother were astonished to hear her speaking in tongues.

You see, even though my mother was born in South Dakota, she was the daughter of immigrants. German was her first language. She learned English only when she went to public school.

In her younger years, being a German was not something to be proud of, and speaking German made people suspicious of your loyalties. So she determined not to speak her native tongue. Not at home, not in public. It was her secret. But like most secrets, it was eventually found out.

Of course, lots of people have secrets, and many of them are not the kind that can cause laughs and well-placed discomfort for knuckleheads. Many of those closely held secrets would cause us great shame and embarrassment if they were known.

A friend of mine once spent time in prison for smuggling drugs. Ironically the bust and prison time took place after he had converted to Christianity and had abandoned any association with the drug trade. It simply took awhile for the government to connect all the dots with enough evidence to arrest him for what he *had* done.

Years later, now a family man running a very successful business, a devout believer and active member of his church, he quietly agonized with me as he tried to decide if he should tell his kids that he was a felon who had spent time in prison . . . before the teens picked up some hint of it from some other source.

Eventually, he decided to talk to his teenage children about his experiences, but not without great fear that he would lose their respect (a fear that proved unfounded).

The Bible records Jesus saying some absolutely fascinating things about secrets. He told His followers:

> There is nothing concealed that will not be disclosed, or hidden that will not be made known. What you have said in the dark will be heard in the daylight, and what you have whispered in the ear in the inner rooms will be proclaimed from the roofs (Luke 12:2-3, *NIV*).

This is pretty darn spooky stuff. Nobody talks much about this in the Christian circles I run in, but perhaps we should. It means that someday it will all come out—the deeds, the motives, the thoughts, the under-the-table deals, the stupid and foolish things said in quiet, hushed tones, the backbiting, backstabbing and betrayals . . . all known.

I, for one, am not looking forward to that day.

Don't get me wrong, I think transparency is great, but I am not sure I want to know everything my friends have ever thought about me, let alone have it shouted from the rooftops of heaven. And I sure as heck don't relish the idea of having to entertain everyone gathered in eternity with some kind of video presentation of all my private thoughts, words and actions.

Perhaps it appears as if this would be interesting, seeing everyone starkly exposed. But it seems to me that it would be more like the first time that I, as a young kid, surfed in front of the famous nude beach called Black's Beach. I walked down the beach thinking that a whole beach of naked people might be a fascinating thing to behold; but I left totally convinced that some things are better left to the imagination.

Jesus was a master at ripping off the façades people erected to hide the secret of who they really were. Take, for instance, the gospel story in John 4.

Jesus to the woman: "Go get your husband."

Woman to Jesus: "Uh, um, I don't have a husband."

Jesus to the woman: "Nicely put. Actually you seem to burn through husbands; what's the current count . . . five? And the guy you are shacking up with now, well we aren't even going to dignify him by calling him a husband, are we?"

Woman to Jesus: "Hey, I got an idea, let's talk theology."

Jesus not only knows our dark secrets, but He also knows those secrets that hide wounds or hurts we would never bring up. Before we even reach out to touch the hem of His garment He knows we are bleeding.

He knows our disappointments, dashed dreams, our unhealed injuries and our despair.

I have come to realize that part of the process of the journey, what comes with trailing behind Christ, is to slowly become more frank, honest and transparent about those things that are going to be found out anyhow.

There are no secrets in the presence of God, so why try to hide things? Just look at how things worked out for those who in some strange kind of mental gymnastics somehow thought they could pull a fast one on the Creator.

The Israelites tried to sneak off and throw up shrines and pillars dedicated to some wooden god and got swept away for their efforts (see 2 Kings 17). Or consider the unhappy fate of Achan, who secretly stashed away loot that he was not supposed to touch and paid for it with his life (see Josh. 7). Ugly.

My personal hero in the area of transparency is a muscular big-wave surfer named Aaron. This hulk of a man is a fairly recent addition to God's family, and to call his pre-conversion life "checkered" would be a considerable understatement. Aaron was a walking train wreck, and once Jesus pulled him out of the rubble, he became determined to fight against the tentacles that wanted to drag him back to his old life.

On his own, Aaron decided that the *only* way to be free of these demons was to become 100 percent transparent and honest about his temptations and failings. And the truth is, Aaron, the novice

Christian, is the most honest, crystal-clear man I know.

Aaron called me as I was pecking away this chapter. He wanted to tell me that he was tempted to start looking at a porn site.

This would seem to be wonderful timing for a chapter with this subject matter, but the truth is, Aaron calls all the time and tells me things that most people would never fess up to.

He says he has to do it to be free . . . and I believe him. Maybe we all need to do a little more confessing and admitting to things that our pride would rather keep hidden.

It is my prayer that at the end of my earthly journey I might be so transparent, so real and genuine and so much the same in private life as I am in the public eye that the heavenly video show of the secret things in my life will be short and really, really boring.

Let us draw near to God with a sincere heart in full assurance
of faith, having our hearts sprinkled to cleanse us from
a guilty conscience and having our bodies washed with
pure water. Let us hold unswervingly to the hope we profess,
for he who promised is faithful.

Hebrews 10:22-23, *NIV*

For there is nothing hidden that will not be disclosed, and nothing
concealed that will not be known or brought out into the open.

Luke 8:17, *NIV*

But the man who loves God is known by God.

1 Corinthians 8:3, *NIV*

Now we see but a poor reflection as in a mirror;
then we shall see face to face. Now I know in part;
then I shall know fully, even as I am fully known.

1 Corinthians 13:12, *NIV*

27

A SCARY GOSPEL

I live a safe, comfortable life.

There are no bars on my doors or windows. Indeed, where I live is so safe that the door remains unlocked almost all of the time. I leave my keys in the car visor.

There are no gangs around here, no graffiti, no soldiers or cops hanging out on the corner. There are no missiles landing in my neighborhood or people planting bombs in the road.

My actions are not monitored, my phone is not bugged and my emails are not screened.

I can speak my mind or even put my message on a placard and march up and down the street without dread of being arrested.

I am very grateful for the opportunity to live without fear or oppression, and I honestly hope and pray that what I experience would become normal life for the whole world.

But as I read the Gospels, I become aware that the simple, uncomplicated, safe life that I have could likely be an anomaly and is not an absolute guarantee. In fact, the guarantee from the Scriptures is somewhat the opposite. Here is just a small sample:

In this world you will have trouble. But take heart! I have overcome the world (John 16:33, *NIV*).

They are going to throw you to the wolves and kill you, everyone hating you because you carry my name. And then, going from bad to worse, it will be dog-eat-dog, everyone at each other's throat, everyone hating each other (Matt. 24:9-10, *THE MESSAGE*).

You're blessed when your commitment to God provokes persecution. The persecution drives you even deeper into

God's kingdom. Not only that—count yourselves blessed every time people put you down or throw you out or speak lies about you to discredit me. What it means is that the truth is too close for comfort and they are uncomfortable. You can be glad when that happens—give a cheer, even!—for though they don't like it, I do! And all heaven applauds. And know that you are in good company. My prophets and witnesses have always gotten into this kind of trouble (Matt. 5:10-12, *THE MESSAGE*).

If you find the godless world is hating you, remember it got its start hating me. If you lived on the world's terms, the world would love you as one of its own. But since I picked you to live on God's terms and no longer on the world's terms, the world is going to hate you. When that happens, remember this: Servants don't get better treatment than their masters. If they beat on me, they will certainly beat on you (John 15:18-20, *THE MESSAGE*).

Okay, then.

Those few verses alone are enough to give one pause about enlisting as a Christian. The gospel in its entirety is pretty scary.

To be honest, even though I wear my faith on my sleeve, I have never really been persecuted. I have lived in a bubble of protection.

I suppose I could fly to Saudi Arabia and start preaching about Jesus on a street corner . . . that oughta pop the bubble, but in everyday life I feel safe and secure.

But while I am aware that the bubble potentially could be popped at any moment, I stand in awe of those who knowingly face the full fury of what Jesus promised would be coming our way.

Their faith costs them something. Mine, in comparison, costs me nothing.

I have had the honor of meeting a few of the remarkable people who have suffered horribly for their faith and somehow managed to survive. As a young man, I had sit-down conversations with a diminutive Dutch woman named Corrie ten Boom who was sent to a death camp for hiding Jews, and an animated Romanian preacher named Richard Wurmbrand who suffered under both the Nazis and the Communists.

Their stories both horrify and amaze me. In my cushy, safe life, I wonder if I could possibly bear up under the cruelty, stress and hatred visited upon these saints.

In some cases, the cost of following Jesus is the stuff of incredibly hard dilemmas and decisions. People who muster up the faith and courage to make godly decisions should be the personalities we celebrate. They should be the heroes we tell our children to emulate.

One of my all-time heroes is someone you probably have never heard of but should have.

Her name was Irena Gutowna. She was the mistress of a Nazi major . . . and a devout Christian. (Yes, I know that you are thinking that there seems to be a conflict of ethics here.) I think the story of what putting her faith into action cost her is worth retelling.

Irena sat fidgeting on the pew of the Chopin Street Catholic church (she was a believing Catholic) in Ternopol, Ukraine. She was waiting for her turn in the confessional booth, and she had time to think about the events and hard choices that brought her to this point.

When Irena was 21 years old, World War II had raged into her Polish town. The stately young blonde had been in nursing school but was drafted by the Polish army to treat wounded soldiers. While working near the front, the town she was in was overrun by Russian soldiers, who at that time were in cahoots with the Germans.

They viciously raped her.

Hospitalized in Ternopol, she recovered from her trauma and was actually sitting in church when the winds of war changed again. Hitler betrayed the Russians, the German army stormed into East Poland, into the Ukraine, into Ternopol and into the very church where Irena sat, seizing any able-bodied parishioner for forced labor. Irena was taken by the Germans that day and ended up working in an ammunitions factory.

Irena's faith was put to the test day after day in the brutal occupation of the Nazi regime. She became eyewitness to the horrors of the Holocaust as it began to unfold in the streets around her.

One day, Irena saw a group of SS men raid a home and drag out the occupants, among them a baby and its mother. As Irena watched in shock, a Nazi officer picked up the infant, shot it and hurled the lifeless child to the ground next to the wailing mother, and then shot the mother too.

Irena's soul was seared by these monstrous acts. She had a crisis of faith and blamed God for allowing such a thing to take place.

"I prayed to God," she said: "*I do not believe in You! You are a figment of my imagination! How can You allow such a thing to happen?*"

The next day Irena had a change of heart. She returned to her knees and prayed: "*Forgive me, I don't know what I am talking about. Thy will be done.*"

During her work as a forced laborer, Irena's job was changed to serve German officers as a waitress in their private club as well as to be the manager for laundry services.

The laundry made use of Jews brought in from concentration camps, and during this Irena made friends with Jewish men and women who had survived the liquidation of their people because they were still useful as slaves for the Nazis.

As a waitress at the officers' club, the pretty blonde Irena also attracted the attention of Nazi big shots, one of whom, a major in the German army, took a fancy to Irena and arranged to have her transferred to his villa as a maid.

Irena knew from hearing conversations at the officers' club (she spoke fluent German) that the noose was about to be tightened around the necks of the few remaining Jews in Ternopol, and she became determined to do whatever she could to save those who had worked with her in the laundry.

Under the nose of the German officer for whom she was a maid, Irena smuggled a dozen Jews into the basement of the villa where she worked and lived. When the major went to work each day, Irena would carefully lock all of the doors and bring her charges up into the house to eat and bathe.

It was an extremely dangerous game, played out right under the nose of the German officer.

But one day Irena forgot to lock the front door and the major returned unexpectedly to find Irena and two of the Jewish women standing in the kitchen. He began to shake with emotion and then spun around and walked out of the kitchen. Irena chased after him and pleaded for mercy.

"Irena! What in God's name have you done to me!" shouted the major, in a voice so loud that the Jews hiding in the basement could hear.

"They are innocent. They've done nothing. Don't turn them in. I beg you! I know you are a good man!" Irena pleaded

The major would hear no more and stormed out of the house in spite of Irena's tears and beseeching.

Irena quickly made escape plans for her wards and steeled herself for the worst.

When the major returned late that evening he was drunk.

In the morning, he called Irena to his room and made her a proposition. She could keep her two friends (he knew nothing of the other 10 Jews quivering in the basement), but she would be required to give him her body in return.

Irena consented.

Later that year, fidgeting in church, Irena waited for her turn in the confessional booth. When she slid in, she quietly confided to the priest that she had become the mistress of a German officer in order to save the lives of her Jewish friends.

"My child, it is a mortal sin," said the confessor priest.

"But, Father, if I don't do this, 12 people will lose their lives," Irena politely objected.

But the priest would not give her absolution.

Irena left the church without the blessing of the priest, but confident of God's approval. "I believe I have God's blessing," she said. "I was never more sure of it."

At the end of the war, after changing hands several times, the city of Ternopol was finally liberated. The Germans left, and Irena's Jews came out of hiding.

Irena eventually married and emigrated from Poland to California.

She refused to talk about the war for decades. But in her later years, after hearing people deny the reality of the Holocaust, she began to speak to anyone who would listen to what she had witnessed.

Irena went to her Lord peacefully in 2003.

Her Jewish friends told everyone they met about the sacrifice this Christian woman had made for them, and in 1982, she was honored with the title of *Righteous Among the Nations* by the country of Israel.

Women like Irena are the heroes of the Christian faith. Their bravery, compassion and incredible personal sacrifice made in order to live out the teaching of Christ should put their stories on the back of every cereal box in America; the soundtrack of their testimonies should be included on every iPod sold.

I often wonder if my safe life has made me so soft that I would have a collapse of courage if suddenly I faced conditions as Irena did. (Most of these heroes say you cannot predict what you will do until you find yourself in the middle of the situation, and they are very gracious to those who lost their nerve.)

I pray that I will get a pass from the heavy, gut-wrenching results cautioned as a possibility for being a follower of Jesus.

And I promise that I will never take for granted or be ungrateful for the safe, soft, free world I have been privileged to live in.

I could go on and on, but I've run out of time. There are so many more—Gideon, Barak, Samson, Jephthah, David, Samuel, the prophets. . . . Through acts of faith, they toppled kingdoms, made justice work, took the promises for themselves. They were protected from lions, fires, and sword thrusts, turned disadvantage to advantage, won battles, routed alien armies. Women received their loved ones back from the dead. There were those who, under torture, refused to give in and go free, preferring something better: resurrection. Others braved abuse and whips, and, yes, chains and dungeons. We have stories of

*those who were stoned, sawed in two, murdered in cold blood;
stories of vagrants wandering the earth in animal skins, homeless, friendless, powerless—the world didn't deserve them!—making their way as best they could on the cruel edges of the world.*

Hebrews 11:32-38, *THE MESSAGE*

Though he slay me, yet will I hope in him.

Job 13:15, *NIV*

28

WHERE IS THE STING?

All of us are aware that someday our journey will end. We will no longer be traveling to the destination but will be there. The final passageway we cross is called death.

Most of us find it morbid to dwell on this subject and, in particular, to dwell on the subject of our own death. We get a weird feeling inside when a parent or spouse starts to talk about his or her own demise. "Aw, don't go on about that!" we say. "You're gonna outlive us all!" And we hope this will shut them up. Death is something that we accept intellectually but don't want to acknowledge emotionally.

Some people get cocky, as if their death is trivial, a walk in the park or like they eat death for breakfast every day. I suppose cocky is better than terrified.

Pundits point out that we are saturated in death. We watch TV shows and movies where (fictional) death is constant; we play video games designed to graphically wipe out our opponent; and we view the news programs showing places that have bombs going off, children starving and disasters sweeping away thousands of lives. But none of these things feel *real* to us. There is no sting to these deaths, fictional or real.

But then death sneaks up close to us. We are shocked and flabbergasted to find that our friend, our family member or our close acquaintance has suddenly died. This can be true even if we and our loved one have been warned that his or her passing is imminent. Death is not supposed to get this personal.

I have always liked that John Bunyan allowed Christian, the central character in the book *Pilgrim's Progress,* to panic when he came to the river that symbolized death, which he had to cross to enter the Celestial City.

The poor guy starts to freak out. He runs around trying to find some other way across. When that option is ruled out he becomes desperate to discover an easy way across the river. He wants a nice death, the same kind I envision for myself; you have a delicious meal, hug your kids good night and crawl into bed snuggling up to your wife, feeling fit as a fiddle. Then sometime in the middle of the night you simply slip across the river. They find you in the morning with a smile on your face, your passage peaceful and painless and your life full of years.

Bunyan would have none of that for his finale. He forced Christian to plunge deep into dark, suffocating waters. The poor man was gasping, terrified, and had pretty much lost all the faith that he had accumulated during his long sojourn.

Of course the character Hopeful finally grabbed Pilgrim and kept his head above water for the passage . . . but barely.

I have watched believers die. Some of them whipped across that river as if on water skis; others were dragged across it slowly, torturously, submerged in pain and confusion, clinging and then loosing their grip on brother Hopeful.

One of my friends is an emergency room physician. He has seen more passing than anyone I have ever known. He told me that he could almost always tell if someone has died, even before the machines they are hooked to begin to sound. "It's in their eyes," he said. "The life goes right out of their eyes. When you've been around it for a while, you can see it."

If death was all that we had to look forward to as the last verse in our song of life, then I am afraid this would be a very depressing chapter.

But I believe I will beat death. I believe that the second the life goes out of my eyes, my new set of eyes will light up with all the data transferred to a more advanced and efficient model. You see, I believe in heaven.

I *do not* believe in the common cartoon kind of heaven, with clouds, harps, robes, halos, wings and pearly gates. Images that I think are used very effectively by the enemy to paint a nerdy, unappealing picture of heaven while pushing a sweaty, lusty, naughty and somewhat enticing picture of hell.

I believe that heaven will be more real than earth. The sharpest, clearest, most poignant joys we experience here will be faintly discernable as mere shadow in contrast with the most insignificant pleasure of heaven.

Unlike a lot of people, I don't think that those who have made the journey before me are waiting around for me to show up, nor are they peering over the edge of a cloud, checking out my progress. And this may sound kind of odd, but I don't think anybody is waiting for me at all.

Now, I am just guessing when I say this, but I figure that since God doesn't operate on our timeline but operates outside of time and space, where all watches are set to "now," when I step off the timeline into His presence will be (in God's time economy) the exact same time when my mother, my friend Jim, my yet-to-be-born grandchild, C. S. Lewis, William Tyndale, Saint Francis of Assisi, Augustine and the apostle Paul will step into His presence. (You may have to think about this one for a while, and it is only a guess. If it is not helpful to you, forget about it.)

I do know that whatever God has up His sleeve is beyond the ability of humans to even imagine or describe (in spite of the apostle John's noble effort in the book of Revelation). And it fills me with fascination, and it bleeds away much of my apprehension about crossing that river.

It may not sound like much to you as you thumb through these pages in the comfort of your own death-free world. (I know that death has not been terribly close to you recently, because if it had, you would surely be reading other more useful works than this book.) But someday you will cling with all you are worth to the assurance of the resurrection power of Jesus and the reality of continued life across the river.

My friend Chris was able to enjoy a respite from ministry by touring Civil War battle sites with his 20-year-old daughter Paige who, like her father, loved history. He had no idea that within days of returning from that father/daughter trip, Paige would perish in a fiery car crash a few miles from their home.

There is nothing that can be worse to a parent than to lose a child, especially in the flower of his or her life. To add to the agony was the fear that his daughter suffered greatly in her last minutes.

Friends and family quickly surrounded Chris and his wife, Rebecca, but this doesn't take away the pain. "Grief is not linear, but circular," Chris was to say later, "and a loved one is remembered daily as a hundred different things bring them into view."

There is only one thing to hold on to, only one thing that makes the unbearable able to be borne: the promise, no, the fact of heaven.

Chris and Rebecca need heaven to be real. If not now, then someday you and I will need heaven to be real, not only for the loved ones whose journey has led them into the dark river but for our own crossing.

It has been said that God never creates a need that He doesn't also provide a satisfaction for. He creates hunger, but He also creates food; He creates creativity, but He also creates a means to express it. He creates an environment where death and sorrow are allowed to exist (I don't believe for a second that He created death or sorrow, but that is a theological point that isn't for this discussion), and He has created a solution to beat that death and end sorrow.

I have come to the point in my journey where I do not fear the prospect of death, but I do have to admit that I am none too pleased about the river.

In a small way, my dad was involved in the creation of the first Disneyland. Because of that I got to be one of the first visitors. Nobody actually knew what to expect; there had never been an amusement park like it. There were only promises, advertisements and a few rumors from those who claimed to be in the know.

But I have to tell you, the second I went through the turnstiles, all apprehension and weariness from the long car ride instantly evaporated in the magical glory of the kingdom that Walt Disney dreamed up.

Just imagine the magical place that the King of kings has come up with! It takes a lot of the sting out of getting there.

At the same moment and in the same way, we'll all be changed. In the resurrection scheme of things, this has to happen: everything perishable taken off the shelves and replaced by the imperishable, this mortal replaced by the immortal. Then the saying will come true: Death swallowed by triumphant Life! Who got the last word, oh, Death? Oh, Death, who's afraid of you now?

1 Corinthians 15:52-55, *THE MESSAGE*

"Pay close attention now: I'm creating new heavens and a new earth. All the earlier troubles, chaos, and pain are things of the past, to be forgotten. Look ahead with joy. Anticipate what I'm creating: I'll create Jerusalem as sheer joy, create my people as pure delight. I'll take joy in Jerusalem, take delight in my people: No more sounds of weeping in the city, no cries of anguish; no more babies dying in the cradle, or old people who don't enjoy a full lifetime; one-hundredth birthdays will be considered normal—anything less will seem like a cheat. They'll build houses and move in. They'll plant fields and eat what they grow. No more building a house that some outsider takes over, no more planting fields that some enemy confiscates, for my people will be as long-lived as trees, my chosen ones will have satisfaction in their work. They won't work and have nothing come of it, they won't have children snatched out from under them. For they themselves are plantings blessed by GOD, *with their children and grandchildren likewise* GOD-*blessed. Before they call out, I'll answer. Before they've finished speaking, I'll have heard. Wolf and lamb will graze the same meadow, lion and ox eat straw from the same trough, but snakes—they'll get a diet of dirt! Neither animal nor human will hurt or kill anywhere on my Holy Mountain," says* GOD.

Isaiah 65:17-25, *THE MESSAGE*

29

EXPENDABLE

I get kicks out of historical stuff. A lot of my friends know this fact and so they often recommend or drop off books they think I will enjoy or bring me trinkets of historical value. One well-meaning friend even brought me a rock about the size of my fingernail.

"What's this?" I said.

"It's a piece of the Coliseum," she beamed, with no apparent sense of irony that it would take only a few hundred years for the Coliseum to disappear if tourists chipped off little pieces to take back to their history buff friends.

"I knew you liked old stuff, so when we went to Rome, I broke this off for you."

"Thanks!" I said, figuring that someday a good earthquake will turn the Coliseum to dust, so stressing over a little fragment of it broken off by my kind but knuckleheaded friend wasn't likely to make much of a difference at this point. (Although I may try to superglue it back on if I ever make it to Rome.)

Enjoying history ultimately means reading quite a bit of stuff about military adventures, and I find this dimension of humanity (and inhumanity) to be curiously fascinating.

Among the heroic, poignant and tragic stories offered up throughout the ages, the ones that bother me the most are the examples of leaders who see the men under them as expendable pawns—men whose lives can be brokered as "acceptable losses" in order to reach some objective a bit faster or make the stars on some general's lapel shine brighter.

These leaders seem callous, perhaps out of sad necessity or perhaps out of coldness and arrogance, to the fact that the soldiers whose lives are traded for some experiment are living, breathing creatures such as themselves, who have entrusted their lives to the cause, believing they would not be unnecessarily wasted.

One such fascinating story is that of Alexander the Great who in his great sweep to conquer the world came to a city buttoned up and ready for a long siege, the leaders inside refusing to surrender.

According to the account passed down to us, Alexander ordered his troopers to line up single file on the top of a huge cliff that overlooked the city.

As the leaders ensconced in the city looked on, Alexander gave the order for his troopers to march forward. They did so one after another, and because Alexander had not issued the order to halt, when the men got to the cliff edge they stepped off into oblivion.

After a dozen or so of his men had stepped off to their death, Alexander gave the halt order and turned his attention again to the leaders on the wall, who after a quick conference surrendered the city without a fight, deciding that any commander who had such fear and respect from his men was invincible.

Kind of a cool story, but I can't help feeling sorry for the first dozen guys in line. I want to think that Alexander loaded the deck by putting men with terminal diseases or injuries up front; but from what I read about this mad Greek, I doubt it.

There are hints that God expends His followers for some grander cause. Consider poor Uriah the Hittite, cuckolded and set up for death by his king, so that generations could have a good object lesson on lust and lying as well as some intensely anguished psalms.

Or how about Minnie Vautrin, the heroic missionary to China, who bravely went toe to toe with Japanese soldiers during the rape of Nanking? Through the courage of Minnie and a few Western friends, she managed to save 20,000 Chinese civilians from slaughter only to suffer from an emotional collapse shortly afterwards (in what we now recognize as Post Traumatic Stress Syndrome) during which she ended her own life.

The Chinese consider her a saint, but she was expended as a result.

While I knew about generals assuming that men were expendable for whatever cause they were fighting, and had some hints from the Bible that God might once in a while use similar devices,

I never thought that He might use the same tactics on me. But now I wouldn't put it past Him; you see, I once felt like one of those consumable people.

I offered myself up to God to use in full-time ministry, and my reward was to not only be denied but to be thrown lock, stock and barrel into a world that I considered abhorrent, sickening and absolutely bewildering.

It may be important to offer up some backstory here.

I came of age in an interesting but extremely unique little world. I was a hardcore surf kid who lived, ate and breathed in the small but intensely competitive world of other hardcore surfers. The early manifestation of that world was almost exclusively male. And to this day, while there are more and more women involved in the sport, like most other extreme sports, men still dominate.

It was, and still is, a world with virtually zero tolerance for male homosexuals. (There are no known gay men in pro surfing, nor are there any openly gay surfers sponsored by any surf gear manufacturers; in their own words, this would be "death" to their products.) Ironically, there have been a few fairly closeted lesbian women surfers on the pro circuit, which simply fuels the misogynist view that women don't really belong in the sport.

I grew up with no exposure to even the idea of homosexuality except for the rough jokes that guys make . . . which, to be honest, suited me just fine.

Finding Jesus did not change this part of my world. I simply infiltrated my faith into the world of water sport in which I lived.

Eventually, I decided to offer whatever abilities and talents I had to God in full-time service. The prevailing attitude among Christians was that this was somehow a higher calling than deciding to become a truck driver or salesman. (This is a viewpoint I no longer subscribe to, I should add. We probably need committed Christian salesmen and truck drivers as much or more than we do pastors.)

There was an idea, implied rather than taught, that in trade for a life of overwork and poverty doing ministry, God would somehow make you happier and more honored than the rest of humanity.

So, off I plodded to Bible school, figuring that when I returned, the doors of ministry opportunity would swing open for an anxious young buck who bristled with intensity, energy and a desire to work with young people.

Wrong, wrong, wrong.

I came home to find that nobody was interested in me. I was too young, had no experience and looked too much like one of those rascally beach guys. (Imagine that!)

The rent was coming due (again!), and out of money, with no prospect of ministry employment, I desperately needed a job. A surf buddy informed me that he was leaving his "cherry" part-time job, which, according to him, entailed driving around delivering flowers to appreciative women.

It was something that I figured I could do for a little while until all these churches that so desperately needed a youth worker woke up to the fact that I was available and willing.

I met with one of the owners of the flower shop and applied for the position of delivery boy. I recall being intrigued by the rich smell of the shop (I had never been in a flower shop before), but the interview was uneventful and I was quickly hired.

The next day, while my friend was training me in the nuances of hauling around flowers, I met the *other* owner.

He seemed warm, friendly and . . . uh, um, different—girly even.

I mentioned it to my buddy, who tossed his head back and laughed.

"Didn't I tell you?" he asked

"Tell me what?"

"The guys who own the flower shop are gay!" (He used a different word than "gay.")

I was dumbfounded. This was not what I had in mind. I was supposed to be serving Christ by chasing kids, not being in the employ of a couple of men who slept in the same bed.

I was not particularly homophobic. I had no more phobia of homosexuals than I did of aliens. I had never (to my knowledge) met either but would prefer not to. Now I was dunked into an environment that scorched at everything that seemed "normal" to me.

I was the only male worker who was straight, and I found to my surprise that these men, in many ways, acted just like other guys I knew: always on the hunt, constantly making jokes and comments loaded with sexual innuendos. It was just that the object of their thoughts and comments was other guys, not girls.

To be honest, it creeped me out.

Actually, I was creeped out a lot working that job.

I was in my physical prime and often felt the sensation of leering eyes watching me as I watered plants in the patio or loaded flowers in the truck. (I actually understood what girls must feel like when guys give their bodies the ol' eye-lock.)

Part of my job was to open the mail, sort out the trash from bills and incoming checks. Every once in a while I would open an envelope to have a sheaf of homosexual pornography fall into my lap as I jumped up and yelped in disgust.

I found that the homosexual community was fairly tight knit and my employers made it a habit to always announce to their friends who waltzed into the shop (and I use the word "waltzed" with some accuracy here) that the young guy trying to load up deliveries was their token straight guy who does *not* want to be touched or harassed.

Frankly, it was like going to work in the twilight zone every day. My only respite from the weird world was when I got on the road or left for home.

And I was miserable.

This job was only supposed to be a temporary sojourn to bring in some cash while God opened up the doors of ministry; but the months passed, and God had seemingly forgotten me.

I hung in there the best I could. It was an uncomfortable and sordid place to work; yet in time, over small bits of conversation, I managed to explain that I was a follower of Jesus. This made for even more humor as I was now the "straight Jesus boy" that was hired to work for what *they* referred to as "a shop of queens."

"This is funny, Lord, great joke!" I prayed. "You can get me out now."

There was no answer. No nibble of any other opportunity to work in anything that even vaguely resembled ministry.

As bizarre as my workplace was, I actually grew to like and, for the most part, enjoy my employers and co-workers. I found that the old adage about hating the sin but loving the sinner wasn't just spiritual window dressing; it was actually possible to do. I was (and still am) absolutely revolted at the sin, but I developed care, compassion and yes, love, for the people I worked with.

It came about slowly and not of my design. They were witty, intelligent, warm, often comedic about their sexuality, and as mixed-up as can be. It seems that the trick to the adage is that you need to spend a lot of time in the company of sinners in order to be able to love them.

Months turned into a year, then more. I would trudge off to this job in the netherworld for half a day and then work for free as a volunteer youth worker assistant in my home church.

My prayers took on the sound of the most whiney of the psalms: "Rescue me, O Lord" was usually how they started.

For all practical purposes of being a full-time youth worker, God had abandoned me.

I became resigned to my fate.

One afternoon, as I took my last load of deliveries to the truck, one of my employers asked if I could come to work an hour or so earlier the next day.

"Sure," I replied.

The morning was crisp with cold, and the foggy ocean haze was still clinging to the coastline as I arrived at work.

There was nothing to do, so I picked up a broom and swept around while my boss leaned on the counter and talked to me.

An hour later his lover arrived, and I went about my regular work.

That afternoon I was asked to come in early again the next day.

It was a repeat of the previous morning except this time the conversation began to take a more serious turn, a distinctly spiritual turn.

I can still recall exactly how our conversation ended.

"You know, the things we are talking about may conflict with the lifestyle you are living," I said.

My boss looked at me as if I were an idiot.

"Don't you think I know that?" he said. "Don't you think I have been weighing that for all these months?"

I nodded in dumb assent. But actually, I had no clue he was even interested in spiritual things, and the discussions that had come up while I was at work always seemed designed to try to "tweak the Christian" rather than be part of a dialogue. It came as a thunderbolt to me.

"Do you know anybody who prays?" he asked.

"Yeah, a whole church full of them," I said.

"Well, could you ask them to pray for me?" he spoke quietly.

"You bet!" I replied, although stunned at the thought.

And we did.

The next day my employer told me that he had decided to commit his life to Christ.

Then all hell broke loose.

At 2:00 A.M., my boss, now a brother in Christ, showed up with suitcase in hand at the apartment I shared with five other guys. It seems my newly converted boss broke the news of his freshly found faith just before a scheduled homosexual orgy was about to take place at his house.

He sheepishly asked if he could spend the night on our couch. (He lived with us for a number of weeks.)

I was fired—immediately—and swore at a lot by my other employer who assumed that I was to blame for the explosion in his world.

It was at that point that it became instantly apparent to me that in God's economy, my plans, goals and ambitions were 100 percent expendable. His will for me was to spend over a year and a half submerged in a strange world in order to *change me* and to be His shoehorn in order to encourage my boss to take a step of faith.

It was truly a Damascus Road experience.

I had spent years praying, "God's will be done," and then presuming that my desires were His since they were couched in some kind of spirituality.

I wanted to be working among brothers and sisters in a nice, safe church environment, and He *knew* it would ruin me. I would have become just another believer mouthing about "loving the sinner" but never actually having to do it. I wanted the rank of leading a young flock, but I would not have earned my stripes.

During the whole process, all I did was gripe about it, the sorry-eyed pot complaining to the Potter that his "great potential" was being squandered among the bouquets and pansies.

I felt foolish, humbled, awed and chastened—and ready for any new adventure God wanted to dream up for me, as I was now unemployed.

Almost immediately the phone rang and I was asked if I would consider a position doing youth work with junior high kids.

Go figure.

Oh, and as a postscript, my Christian ex-boss really had a life-transforming change. He left the gay lifestyle behind him, eventually married, became a parent and continues to walk with Christ.

And yes, I understand there is heated debate about whether a person can or should change or modify his or her sexual orientation. My response would simply be, "I don't know, but obviously it seems that sometimes, some people can."

I'll embrace as a brother or sister any believer who is willing to let God change him or her into whatever He wants them to be, regardless of what background they have come from. (We even take lawyers.) There is no part of us that is not, in the end, expendable for His higher purpose.

> *Who in the world do you think you are to second-guess God? Do you for one moment suppose any of us knows enough to call God into question? Clay doesn't talk back to the fingers that mold it, saying, "Why did you shape me like this?" Isn't it obvious that a potter has a perfect right to shape one lump of clay into a vase for holding flowers and another into a pot for cooking beans? If God needs one style of pottery especially designed to show his angry displeasure and another style carefully crafted to show his glorious goodness, isn't that all right?*
> Romans 9:20-23, *THE MESSAGE*

30

THE THEOLOGY OF PINOCCHIO

When my kids were young, I bought the DVD of Walt Disney's version of *Pinocchio* and made them watch it with me. I turned the lights off and the volume up. It brought back sweet memories of movie matinees with sticky floors, greasy popcorn, Jujubes, Black Crows and Milk Duds all washed down with root beer.

My kids have been raised on computer-generated animated films where there is constant breakneck action and the absence of singing flowers. They were underwhelmed with the slow gait of *Pinocchio* and pretty soon wiggled away, leaving me to return to my childhood without them.

I had a terrific time.

I didn't realize until I watched *Pinocchio* as an adult that it had amazingly good theology. It seemed to me that I was watching an allegory on par with the Narnia stories, except that the characters dance.

Sure, every kid could see some of the moral teaching inherent in the film. The point of the whopper-telling puppet's nose extending and blossoming into a limb with complementary bird nest was stated clearly: A lie becomes as clear as the nose on your face.

But there was much I didn't pick up on.

As a kid, I missed the fact that the Blue Fairy was a symbol of the divine: a "God type" as they say in theology classes. It never connected that the boy of wood was assigned a conscience by the divine figure. It never occurred to me that the lack of strings could be a metaphor for free will. I didn't clue in to the pun that said disobedience and rebellion would turn Pinocchio into an ass. I never noticed that it was only when the puppet was willing to die to himself that he found life (courtesy again of the divine touch) as a real little boy. The whole story was about the journey from being a wooden-headed idiot to being made into a real person.

"This is the big story!" I whispered to no one in particular. I wonder if Walt even knew what kind of story he was really telling.

This is our story, yours and mine.

We come into the world through the touch of God, stringless and able to make our own choices but not alone, for the Bible tells us that on our hearts there is written the truth about our maker (see Rom. 1–2). We are appointed a conscience to help us decipher the thoughts of God and prod us in His direction.

But it is a dangerous world, full of clever and charming rogues. We are tempted, lured, and we quickly abandon our squeaking conscience helper for the distractions of Pleasure Island.

Rather than experiencing the pleasure advertised, we soon find ourselves trapped, captured and, to our horror, turning into an ass. Sin takes us away from our dream of being real and turns us into an animal. It takes getting to the place where we will throw our own lives down before God that makes us real.

The whole point of the journey is to help transform us from lumber to flesh, from poser to the real deal, from hidden to transparent.

It seems pretty apparent that in the mathematics of the Kingdom, the more we make the choice to throw down our own will, agenda and self-desire, the more real we become. And the more we choose to keep our own will, agenda and self-desire (however handsomely we disguise it), the more of an ass we become, complete with hoof, long ears and tails.

In other words, by each of those innumerable choices we make each day, we either ascend toward being *real*, a creature unlike our splintery wooden selves, or we descend toward being merely talking animals that dress up nicely and bray with sophistication.

Jesus cast those daily choices in either/or language. We gather the harvest with Him or scatter it to keep Him from having it. We are hot or we are cold in our heart toward Him. We are on His path, following Him on His journey, or we are part of the traffic jam on that famous highway to hell. We serve Him as our exclusive Master or we serve another master.

You can never accuse Jesus of ambiguity.

Those choices that we get to make every day are the ones that sculpt us into someone who is in the likeness of the only real Man to ever walk the earth, or they corrupt us into something we were never created to become. These are rarely the big earth-shattering decisions and choices that would carve the dimensions of our life in a tidal wave instant. These are the small, seemingly insignificant decisions that, like a constant drip, recast us in beauty or simply erode us.

It is how you respond to the annoying guy at work that is a choice you must face. It is what you decide to do with your bonus check; whether to fabricate an excuse or tell the truth; whether to lay aside or hold on to your anger, even anger you have a right to; whether to forgive the slight of another or cling to bitterness; whether to show on your countenance obvious disdain for a group of tattooed, face-studded kids or give them a warm smile. It is whether you stop and listen when you have lots of work to get done; it is in something as small as a tenor of encouragement instead of a tone of criticism.

I don't know about you, but I have a much easier time making right choices in the big things than I do in the little stuff. I am not as likely to be a thief as I am a glutton. (Not for food, mind you, but for the newest electronic gadgets.) I am not as likely to murder a person I don't care for as I am to simply snub them.

Genuine Christianity is usually found in the choices we make in the minutia and nuances of life. It is around these small things that our realness takes shape.

One thing is for sure: What we currently are will, like wooden puppets, someday burn up in a cosmic fire in which only that which is real will survive.

That is good theology even if it comes from a cartoon puppet.

Generous in love—God, give grace! Huge in mercy—wipe out my bad record. Scrub away my guilt, soak out my sins in your

*laundry. I know how bad I've been; my sins are staring
me down. You're the One I've violated, and you've seen it all,
seen the full extent of my evil. You have all the facts before you;
whatever you decide about me is fair. I've been out of step with
you for a long time, in the wrong since before I was born.
What you're after is truth from the inside out. Enter me, then;
conceive a new, true life.*

Psalm 51:1-6, *THE MESSAGE*

31

END THOUGHTS

Each of our lives is an unwinding story. As we accumulate years, we find our journey containing both drama and subtlety. We tend to remember the drama and consider those moments pivotal, but I sometimes think that the real shaping of our lives is in the subtlety.

The choices we make, usually in the minutia, to follow Christ where He would lead, or to custom design our own path will ultimately determine the narrative of our story. In the end, our lives may serve as an inspiration to others or they may serve as a warning.

My idea for this work was to spin from the fabric and experiences of my life, threaded with humor and a moment or two of soul-baring, some kind of hope and encouragement for your travels. My desire is that something you have read within these pages has given you hope that:

You are not alone.
Others of us have those same thoughts and feelings.

You are not that weird.
Our faith is often convoluted, inconsistent and conflicted.

You will make it.
You still have a long way to go, but by hanging on to Jesus, your faith, understanding and wisdom will grow, and yes, it is difficult and even baffling at times.

I would like to tell you that the journey gets easier over time, but that would be a half-truth. At the very point that you acclimate and finally get used to the new spiritual altitude, God hollers at you to get up and get moving again.

The question each of us needs to ask ourselves at the end of the day is not, "Did I achieve something great today?" or "How far did I get in my spiritual journey?" but rather, "Did I go forward or backward?" Did I inch toward Jesus in my thoughts and actions? Have I responded to the people God has put in my life in such a way that God is pleased?

I honestly believe that it is not the length of our gait or the mileage of our journey that makes the difference, but the *direction* we are pointed. In terms of reaching the goal of being like Jesus, sprinters and shufflers are, in the end, pretty much the same.

Someday we will get up and take a little baby step, hesitant and weak, in the direction of our Master only to find that we are suddenly hurled to the finish line in the company of all the other sad-sack followers of Jesus, shufflers and improbable disciples.

I'll see you there.